Praise for *Holding Up Your Corner*

"I had been silent too long. As a pastor I knew I had to speak up, but I had no idea how to navigate the complex conversations around race. After reading *Holding Up Your Corner*, I began to feel empowered and equipped to do my part. As a pastor, I now see myself as having a key voice in our community around issues of injustice. This would not have been possible without the story, inspiration, and guidance of F. Willis Johnson."
—Jacob Armstrong, pastor, Providence UMC, Mt. Juliet, TN

"Willis Johnson's words on racial inequality, 'even if it's not our fault, it's our fight,' grabbed me early on and wouldn't let go. This is a rare gem of a book; it opened my eyes, tugged at my heart, and causes me to wrestle with what to do at my own corner. The church has needed this book, and I hope it along with the study guide will become a catalyst for healing, hope, and change in our culture."
—Jim Ozier, New Church Development and Congregational Transformation, North Texas Conference of The United Methodist Church

"Our congregations and communities are crying out for material that can help leaders bridge the divides segregating us by race and class. This is a tremendous tool for leaders of congregations and communities, which I will be putting to great use in my local church and community. This is a must read."
—Joe Daniels, pastor, Emory United Methodist Church, Washington, DC

"*Holding Up Your Corner* is the fresh, practical, theological, user-friendly, and urgent resource for which our churches have been waiting. If every congregation across America utilized this as a church-wide study, the entire atmosphere of countless communities would be transformed."
—Sue Nilson Kibbey, Director of the Office of Missional Church Development, West Ohio Conference of The United Methodist Church

"Willis Johnson is an authentic and prophetic voice for our day."
—Robert Schnase, bishop, Rio Texas Conference of The United Methodist Church; author of *Five Practices of Fruitful Congregations*

"*Holding Up Your Corner* offers practical ways for communities to 'do better.'"
—Kim Jenne, Director of Connectional Ministries, Missouri Annual Conference of The United Methodist Church

"Silence is no longer an option. If you have a passion to engage your community with Christ's reconciling power, this book is for you."
—Rosario Picardo, executive pastor, New Church Development, Ginghamsburg Church, Tipp City, OH

"*Holding Up Your Corner* guides pastors to lead conversations in diverse communities for the development of peace-filled relationships through Christ-centered transformation."
—Robert Farr, bishop, Missouri Conference of The United Methodist Church

"I read *Holding Up Your Corner* with a rising sense of excitement and gratitude. This is what is meant by "equipping the saints" for the work of God in the world. This resource is insightful, intelligent, and inspiring—a gift to all who believe in and struggle for justice grounded in their faith."
—Allan Boesak, South African theologian and activist; Desmond Tutu Chair of Peace, Justice and Reconciliation Studies at Christian Theological Seminary and Butler University, Indianapolis, IN

"This book will change us, if we take it to heart and action. I dare you to read and implement it!"
—Dottie Escobedo-Frank, district superintendent, Desert Southwest Conference of The United Methodist Church

"Willis Johnson is a pastor and a citizen who can speak to anyone and elevate everyone. His call to 'hold up your corner' will motivate readers of all backgrounds to act for racial justice. His clear guides for conversation and action show us how to do the work."
—Eric Liu, CEO of Citizen University; author of *You're More Powerful Than You Think*

"In *Holding Up Your Corner*, F. Willis Johnson astutely shapes an argument for the Christian's responsibility to justice-making."
—Pamela R. Lightsey, Associate Dean, Clinical Assistant Professor, Boston University School of Theology, Boston, MA; author of *Our Lives Matter: A Womanist Queer Theology*

"Racism and racial injustice are a persistent stain in our communities. *Holding Up Your Corner* is a manual—a framework of questions, actions, and models for people of faith and courage, equipping them to engage in the work of tackling these issues."
—Asa J. Lee, Associate Dean for Community Life, Wesley Theological Seminary, Washington, DC

"I guarantee that after reading Willis Johnson you will want to work from your corner to become part of God's work in the world."
—Will Willimon, retired UMC bishop, Professor of the Practice of Christian Ministry, Duke Divinity School, Durham, NC

F. Willis Johnson

HOLDING UP YOUR CORNER

Talking about Race in Your Community

Abingdon Press

Nashville

HOLDING UP YOUR CORNER:
TALKING ABOUT RACE IN YOUR COMMUNITY

Copyright © 2017 by Abingdon Press

All rights reserved.

No part of this work may be reproduced or transmitted in any form or by any means, electronic or me-chanical, including photocopying and recording, or by any information storage or retrieval system, except as may be expressly permitted by the 1976 Copyright Act or in writing from the publisher. Requests for permission can be addressed to Permissions, The United Methodist Publishing House, 2222 Rosa L. Parks Blvd., PO Box 280988, Nashville, TN 37228, or e-mailed to permissions@umpublishing.org.

Library of Congress Cataloging-in-Publication Data has been requested.

ISBN 978-1-5018-3759-3

Scripture quotations unless noted otherwise are from the Common English Bible. Copyright © 2011 by the Common English Bible. All rights reserved. Used by permission. www.CommonEnglishBible.com.

Scripture quotations marked (The Message) are taken from THE MESSAGE. Copyright © by Eugene H. Peterson 1993, 1994, 1995, 1996, 2000, 2001, 2002. Used by permission of NavPress Publishing Group.

17 18 19 20 21 22 23 24 25 26—10 9 8 7 6 5 4 3 2 1
MANUFACTURED IN THE UNITED STATES OF AMERICA

This work is lovingly dedicated to those whose shoulders we stand upon and strivings we celebrate by holding up our corner!

Willis "Bing" Davis is a contemporary artist and educator. He was born in 1937 in Greer, South Carolina, but has studied, taught, and lived in Indiana and Ohio most of his life. He graduated from DePauw University in 1959 and is an inductee in the DePauw University sports hall of fame. He operates a gallery and is involved in community and arts programs in Dayton, Ohio, and across the United States. He serves as President of the Board of Directors of the National Conference of Artists. Davis makes art from found objects and uses mixed media, including photography, drawing, painting, ceramics, and sculpture. He is influenced by ancestral resources and makes African-rooted art such as masks and shrines using African-inspired materials.

Davis met the author of this book in 2015, and the two established a friendship. During the development of this book, Davis created a new work, "Young Warriors with Dancing Sticks," pictured here. It is a photo collage measuring 20" x 16 1/2".

When I saw Rev. F. Willis Johnson standing in the midst of our young brothers and sisters, who were protesting in the streets of Ferguson, MO, I saw an often forgotten African tradition coming forth. I saw a wise elder from the community standing in the middle of pain and sorrow, offering vision, wisdom, spiritual and moral support to the most valuable segment of our community—our youth, our young warriors and nation-builders. —Willis Bing Davis

Davis and the author share a belief that art communicates what cannot be said but what must be understood. Davis is inspired by other art as well. Paul Laurence Dunbar was one of the first African American poets to gain international recognition. His work "We Wear the Mask" is a particular influence on Mr. Davis:

We Wear the Mask

We wear the mask that grins and lies,
It hides our cheeks and shades our eyes, —
This debt we pay to human guile;
With torn and bleeding hearts we smile,
And mouth with myriad subtleties.

Why should the world be over-wise,
In counting all our tears and sighs?
Nay, let them only see us, while
We wear the mask.

We smile, but, O great Christ, our cries
To thee from tortured souls arise.

We sing, but oh the clay is vile
Beneath our feet, and long the mile;
But let the world dream otherwise,
We wear the mask!

—Paul Laurence Dunbar, 1896

More information, including images of Davis's work, can be found at www.bingdavis.tripod.com.

How wonderful it is that nobody need wait a single moment before starting to improve the world.

—Anne Frank

CONTENTS

Contents

Contents

Preface

WHAT HAPPENED
IN MY CORNER

In August 2014, I was serving as the pastor to Wellspring Church in Ferguson, Missouri, when Michael Brown Jr., an unarmed African American teenager, died at the hands of a white police officer. I first found out about the shooting via text message. I initially disregarded friends who were sending me information about what had happened. It was unfortunate to hear about the shooting of a young black man, but it was not unusual. In reflection, I'm disturbed by how comfortable I and others have become hearing about loss of life, and the regular occurrence of a young black man being shot by police officers. Initially, this event didn't derail my day. A few hours later, I was in my home across the way from the Ferguson Police Department when I heard the noise of chanting, hollering, and a general business that wasn't the norm on my sleepy street. I grabbed my comfortable shoes, aware that something was happening. This was the clarion call, that moment, that situation where people realize that everything has not been alright.

In the days following, all hell broke loose in my community. There were demonstrations and protests, vandalism and looting, rubber bullets and tear gas. It was as though a slowly dripping dam had burst open in a deafening torrent of accusations, ill will, distrust, and dissension. As many followed from their living rooms, the news cycle was flooded with images and videos recording the events in Ferguson. However, time is not measured by news cycles, and events are never fully explained in media sound bites. In the days that followed Brown's death, various local efforts to respond and process arose as business as usual stalled and time seemed to stand still.

A few days after Brown's death, I participated in a march led by area clergy. The exercise was intended to bring awareness of clergy persons' displeasure with the circumstances surrounding Michael Brown Jr.'s death, as well as law enforcement's handling of the case thereafter. In addition, we wished to present a visible sign of solidarity with youth and residents of Canfield. In company with other clergy and concerned citizens, we marched from a staging area farther up West Florissant Avenue down to the improvised memorial in Canfield. As marchers attempted to turn at the intersection of West Florissant Avenue and Canfield Drive to go the last few hundred feet, we noticed Ferguson police officers had beaten us there. March organizers were momentarily unsure of what to do.

"Should we keep going?" people asked. "They're obviously waiting for us to get down there." Did they intend to arrest us? Did they recognize we were clergy? Should we continue onward, despite the risks?

In the confusion of should-we-or-shouldn't-we, one of the women demonstrating with us made the first move. She simply sat down—in the middle of the intersection. Within seconds, other young women sat down beside her. Then a dear friend, Ivan Douglas Hicks, whom I had invited to come help with my church's response to the situation, said, "Well, we cannot let the sisters sit down by themselves." So he sat down, pulling me down with him. Suddenly, we had ourselves a sit-in.

This was not my plan for the day. Ministry is like that, isn't it?

As you might expect, after some time the police were ready for us to move. As you might also expect, the young people who anchored the demonstration were not ready to go anywhere. Soon, we went from having Ferguson police officers on the scene to having a few Saint Louis County police officers there, to having a whole lot of county cops staring us down.

I clearly remember thinking, *Okay, we've gotta get up.*

I stood to seek out a few police officers I knew, in hopes of de-escalating the situation. I reminded them we had a state senator with us, but I was met with, "It's out of our hands." The Ferguson police moved back from the intersection—which is when I first saw the tanks.

State Senator Maria Chappelle-Nadal lost it. "We are not moving! We are not moving!"

As an adolescent, I never considered anything I was ready to die for. On that day, at nearly forty years old, I instinctively shifted into self-preservation mode: "Okay . . . They brought tanks. They have guns. They mean business. If they're this brash, and they've already killed one—and they've killed hundreds of others before us—we need not try this one. They already feel they're justified."

But the young people stayed there—sitting in the intersection. I remember the sense of anger and fatigue in the air that day—soon matched with fearlessness. Their attitude was, "If they want to do something to us, they're just going to have to do it."

At one point that afternoon, I found myself standing between demonstrators and a line of cops in their riot gear, and there are photos of me desperately urging and pleading younger demonstrators to back down. I must have been delirious or desperate. In that moment I don't really know what I was trying to do, but I suppose I was hoping to save them. Save them from what is many black parents' greatest fears for our sons and daughters—arrested development or death at the hands of merciless systems. In hindsight it was an action that bordered on stupidity. Incredible stupidity. It was stupid by definition, given it was an act contrary to better judgment. I assumed these anonymous young people would heed the instructions of a self-appointed authority, and, at the same time, that the militarized makeshift municipal militia would regard my black body with no more respect than it had for others. I stood with my back to their shields and batons. A marksman atop the tank pointed a rifle in our direction.

My stupidity was in my urge to save, in the belief that I could somehow save people or salvage the situation. I alone did not have the power to save anyone that day. All any one person can do in moments of crisis like these is respond to the people and the pain present before them. Some have called me brave for placing myself in a situation of perceived danger that day. However, it was not true bravery. I have learned since that bravery occurs when we clearheadedly face injustice that is embedded in us and envelops us, and then make the conscious decision to engage. It is the decision to actively and intentionally open our eyes to our place in systems, open our ears to the pain and hollering of people around us, and open our hearts to one another in order to do justice.

As pastors and church leaders, it may be challenging for us to face injustice, to engage with it, to recognize and name the ways we participate in it. It may be highly uncomfortable for us—even as pastors—to sit with someone who is in pain—pain that is so different from our own—and to understand it, to validate that it is real. But, by and large, we can muster up the courage to do those things; we've been trained in this direction.

But to do justice—that is a much harder thing. Justice requires us to act.

There have been countless moments—from August 2014 until now—when I have found myself wondering if our community would be able to survive the aftermath of Michael Brown's death. Each time that question comes to mind, I sense a clear answer: Surviving isn't enough. When justice is done, we will thrive.

Waiting on the Grand Jury

For more than ninety days—a length of time past expiration for some, not long enough for others—our community lived in suspense while suspicion grew. We awaited the decision of whether a grand jury would indict Darren Wilson, the officer who shot and killed Michael Brown Jr.

In anticipation of the ruling, the Ferguson-Florissant School District and adjacent school districts planned to close schools when the grand jury released its decision. According to reports, the Ferguson Police Department stockpiled teargas, grenades, and other weaponry to use in the event that civil disorder followed a grand jury decision not to indict Wilson. Nearby law enforcement agencies likewise prepared for civil unrest. These were unnerving indicators that law enforcement agencies were preparing a definitive, violent response to civil disorder without allowing for the possibility of other, less-dangerous alternatives. Nowhere in the chaos did we hear voices asking why. Why were the people of Ferguson and our supporters so hurt? Why were we so scared? Why were we so angry?

The announcement and circumstances swirling around it led to civil disorder. Stress and strain caused us to shout; it was not plausible for us to remain silent or shut up in our homes. Predicaments like Ferguson require remonstration. This is true not only in Ferguson; it's true in every place where people are pained and protracted problems persist. This is not an attempt to enter into debate or point fingers, or continue conversations that have been played over and over in the media. For the purpose of this book, for us as pastors and leaders in the church, it doesn't matter who burned the gas station down. What is important is the hurt and hopelessness experienced by so many all over the United States and around our world. What is important is our responsibility to respond, to bring those who are hurting on our corner to the source of hope and healing.

ACKNOWLEDGMENTS

A tremendous debt of gratitude is owed to my wife, Kristina Irene Johnson, for the countless prayers, exhortations, stern reminders, and allowances given toward completion of this work. Much oblige is extended to the Wellspring Church at Ferguson family and the Center for Social Empowerment team I have the privilege of journeying with toward justice and liberation. Special thanks to Constance Stella, Nicki Reinhardt-Swierk, Conner Kenaston, Joshua Manning, and every sojourner met at the intersection of hurt and help. Most of all, to my children and family, words cannot express the joy you have brought to my life. I am grateful for the lessons learned and faith that has developed in me through your gifts and presence. I stand in awe of the resiliency and greatness that reside in each of you. My prayer is that you are inspired by this work as much as you have inspired me.

And let's get a couple things straight, just a little side note—the burden of the brutalized is not to comfort the bystander. That's not our job, alright—stop with all that. If you have a critique for the resistance, for our resistance, then you better have an established record of critique of our oppression. If you have no interest, if you have no interest in equal rights for black people then do not make suggestions to those who do. Sit down.

We've been floating this country on credit for centuries, yo, and we're done watching and waiting while this invention called whiteness uses and abuses us, burying black people out of sight and out of mind while extracting our culture, our dollars, our entertainment like oil—black gold, ghettoizing and demeaning our creations then stealing them, gentrifying our genius and then trying us on like costumes before discarding our bodies like rinds of strange fruit. The thing is though...the thing is that just because we're magic doesn't mean we're not real.

—Jessie Williams, actor and activist
2016 BET Awards

INTRODUCTION

On August 9, 2014, an unarmed, African American teenager was fatally shot by a white police officer. Within three days, our country was shoved into long-overdue conversations about race, police brutality, the militarization of police forces, and injustice of all kinds. My church and community were at the epicenter: Ferguson, Missouri.

In the weeks and months that followed, my colleagues—both clergy and laity—asked the same questions again and again: "What can we do?" and "How do we do it?" We demonstrated peacefully. We contributed toward donuts and coffee for the police, and we poured milk into tear-gassed eyes. Our schools closed, so we cared for our community's kids so their parents could still go to work. These practical measures were helpful, but they didn't get to the heart of the questions: Why is there still injustice, and how is the church supposed to address it?

Our Challenge as Church Leaders

Pastors and other church leaders, along with other people of faith, have come to see the injustice that permeates our communities. Many of these people—especially pastors—understand that they are called to address and correct these injustices. Many wish to speak prophetically about the issues that currently tear at our communal connections. Despite these good intentions, the problems of structural injustice seem irreversible, intractable, and overwhelming. It is difficult to figure out how to begin unwinding those problems.

Additionally, dealing with and addressing injustice requires us to take risks. It is possible that our actions oriented toward justice may not be popular in our places of belonging; they may even push members away from our churches. We may be unfollowed, unfriended, or even harassed digitally by those in our circles. We also fear that we will do or say the wrong thing. A poorly chosen word or a misguided action might make matters worse, increasing tension or sparking a new strain of conflict. We might embarrass our denomination or our congregation. We might humiliate ourselves.

So many of us do not know where or how to begin. We feel poorly equipped, and some of us question our own empowerment. And so, even during times of crisis, pastors and other leaders typically do less than they know they could and should.

What This Book Will (and Will Not) Do

Holding Up Your Corner is an effort to grapple with the complexity of addressing injustice from a faith-rooted perspective. It's aimed at equipping and empowering you, reader, to begin living into that call from God to address and correct injustice in your community. It's important to note, however, that you will not find "Five Simple Steps to Eliminate Injustice in Your Community." There are no five steps. There is nothing simple about any of this. This work is messy. It's potentially dangerous. It may frustrate your superiors. It may offend or alienate your followers. It will require that you reallocate time, energy, and resources toward overlooked ministry opportunities. It will require courage as you're pushed outside of a comfort zone you didn't even know existed.

This book seeks to provide a practical, foundational guide to help you discern your calling to address injustice. You will, I hope, grow in your knowledge of the problems of race and inequity. You will be pressed to examine the embedded structures of privilege in your life and in our society. You will be prompted to observe, identify, and name the complex causes of indifference, violence, and hatred in our society at large and in your particular context.

Holding Up Your Corner should serve as a self-directed process for determining what role to play in your particular location. Please understand, I cannot tell you what to do or how to do it. Each context is unique, and each leader operates from a particular set of circumstances. You must determine the specific strategies and tactics for yourself. This book will prepare you for that work and help you get started.

The Structure of the Book

Holding Up Your Corner is comprised of three parts. The first part provides the foundation and will get you up to speed on this topic. The second part introduces a framework for you to use in considering your own response and faithfully leading others to respond. The third part provides tools and resources, and introduces a powerful next step: *Holding Up Your Corner: Guided Conversations about Race.* This is a "guided" experience for leaders from congregations and communities, aimed at fostering relationships that will lead to change. This next-level, lab-style learning experience was developed in conjunction with the Center for Social Empowerment. My hope is that you will consider facilitating this experience in your own community, at least once. The participant book and DVD are available separately, and a facilitator's guide is available online as a free download.

This book was birthed out of my experiences in Ferguson, so I'll begin with that story. In chapter 2, I'll frame our conversation with an examination of ethical prophetic witness, and I'll introduce the Empathic Model of Transformation (EMT), rooted in the biblical story of the paralytic. In chapters 3–5, I'll unpack EMT into its three components: Acknowledge, Affirm, and Act. You will learn to use personal reflection, the experiences of others, and their God-talk or theology to

1. acknowledge the realities in your own community and your role in both the problem and solutions; to find the places where God's kingdom is not yet overcoming selfishness, injustice, inequality, or the forces of evil;

2. affirm those who have been "othered"[1] in your community, seeking to work in solidarity and to respect the humanity and autonomy of those who are marginalized;

3. act according to your divine call by organizing interventions and activating efforts to address these specific injustices.

---

1. "Other" is anyone who is unlike ourselves. Those whose political perspective and affiliations differ from mine are other. Others are "them" people who live on the opposite side of town or operate outside mainstream culture, particularly Christian culture. In *Fear of the Other: No Fear in Love* retired bishop and professor William Willimon employs a Wesleyan perspective in examining what may be the hardest thing for people of faith to do: keeping and loving the "other" as they are—without any desire for them to become like us.

In each of the EMT chapters, you'll find additional theological grounding and ideas for next steps for you, your congregation, and your community. Each of these chapters includes an example from another leader, demonstrating ways to apply the main ideas of EMT. The chapters conclude with a set of questions for you to ponder on your own, with your team, or with other leaders.

My hope is that your journey through this book will open your eyes, your mind, and, most importantly, your heart to the injustice—the lived trauma or hurt—in your own community. Where there are people, there is injustice, and that is not God's design. It may not be our fault, but it is our fight. Let us do our part by holding up our corners.

What Does "Holding Up Your Corner" Mean?

The phrase "holding up your corner" is derived from a biblical story about four people who take action in order to help another person—literally delivering that person to Christ. For us, "holding up your corner" has meaning in two aspects of our lives today:

First, it refers to our physical and social locations, the places where we live and work, and the communities of which we're a part. These are the places where our assumptions, attitudes, and beliefs have influence on the people around us. When we feel empowered to speak out about the injustice or inequity in our community, we are holding up our corner.

Second, the phrase refers to our actions, the ways we step up to meet a particular problem of injustice or inequity, and proactively do something about it. When we put ourselves—literally—next to persons who are suffering, and enter into their situation in order to bring hope and healing to the person and the situation, we are holding up our corner, just like the four people who held up the corner of the hurting man's mat.

> *"Holding Up Your Corner" refers to (1) our physical and social locations—the places where we live and work, and the communities of which we're a part, where we can use our influence to speak out, and (2) our actions—the ways we step up to meet a particular problem of injustice or inequity, and proactively do something about it.*

Part One
UNMASKING REALITY

Chapter One
REAL TALK

The preacher's task is to describe the world from the Christian point of view, a point of view rooted in biblical narrative and Christian doctrine. The theologian's job, on the other hand, is not to make the gospel credible to the modern world, but to make the world credible to the gospel.

Serving in an urban context requires addressing issues and conditions brought on by economic disparity such as racism, educational dysfunction, cyclical unemployment, incarceration, and genocide. These contexts are often more diverse in terms of race, spiritual and religious practice, and personal orientation. The lived realities of our time demand theological language of practice that wrestles with the complexities of our social lives and systems for the purposes of responding to the reality of intergenerational community. Such language must both attract and attach itself to a new generation committed to sacrificing in order to address and perpetuate faith. We need language and biblically informed theology that meets people where they are, even in the experience of oppression and marginalization.

In these times of polls, squawk boxes, and unsolicited nonqualified sociopolitical commentary, the assumed value of public opinion, groupthink, and consensus is at a premium. Never have we been so technologically advanced, globally connected, and resource rich; yet seemingly so intellectually stagnant and socially repressed. Not since the days of chattel slavery and Jim Crow has this country been so socially nonaccepting of persons exercising intellectually inspired, economically empowered, and culturally conscious awareness. Democratic values and practices no longer encourage individual thinkers, courageous and prophetic leadership, or equitable and sociopolitical exchange. Our judicial system benefits those who have power while steamrolling over the rights of people of color.

Our current late-capitalist economy was predicated on slavery. It continues to require low-wage or free labor, breeding inequality. Its ideals promote a self-made or "bootstrap" mentality that doesn't reflect the lived experiences of many Americans. This system fundamentally takes, rapes, and pimps to ensure security for the rich. The United States of America, a democratic society, was founded on an understanding of government for the people by the people. A system of rules where people are to be duly elected. However, as it exists currently, our political and economic systems are compromised by misrepresentation fueled by political pandering and the influence of special-interest groups and other controlling forces.[1]

The United States possesses an extraordinarily diverse portfolio of natural resources. Our educators and scholars have access to the highest levels of education, technology, and research. Our nation wields tremendous military might. And our cities and towns are vibrant and rich with ethnic and cultural plurality. Yet our nation remains inequitable, oppressive, abusive, and intolerant toward its citizens who put forth independent thought or take righteous action to confront injustice. There exists within our society an issue of both democratic and theocratic rule. The democratic responsibility is to "lift every voice" and the

---

1. For more information about what characterizes late-capitalism, see Fredric Jameson, *Postmodernism, or, the Cultural Logic of Late Capitalism* (Durham: Duke UP, 1991).

"uplift of every block, barrio, and hood." Our democratic responsibility requires us to reexamine misguided, oppressive, and abusive social constructs. Theocratic rule, on the other hand, demands more. It demands that we not only address oppressive systems, but that we work to heal the hurt in our world.

Slavery, segregation, and oppression are undeniably a part of our history. Racial injustice is one of the root causes of economic disparity and social disenfranchisement, as well as political and judicial manipulation and dehumanization. Simply put, black and brown folks are struggling to be free. Talking about God in the face of so much turmoil can be quite the challenge. How do you share the good with someone when they are experiencing so much that is bad? How do you present the light of hope in the darkness of hopelessness? Where is the joy in the midst of sorrow? These are the cries that are heard in the streets, alleyways, churches, schools, homes, and slums of communities all over the world. These are the cries to which we must respond with ethical prophetic witness.

Our God-Talk

Responding to injustice with ethical prophetic witness requires us to be intentional about our theology, or God-talk. Theology is defined as the reflection and dialogue on the interrelatedness of the Christian deity to humanity and creation. Theology is all about figuring out relationships: between God and humanity, God and creation, humanity and creation, and our relationship to the rest of humanity. Our respective God-talk is more than mere explanation of what individuals think and feel toward our deity. It classifies and clarifies the struggle to live out belief as a community. Ultimately, theology is a function of the church. The church's God-talk gives shape and definition to both its constituency and the institution's most fundamental claims and practices.

In this book I will generally avoid dense theological analysis in favor of the practical implications of our theological underpinnings, but it is helpful to examine the difference between embedded and deliberative theology. *Embedded theology* is the theology that we absorb from our families, church experiences, and world. While we are influenced constantly by the world around us, those of us who were raised in church environments likely received our embedded theology through explicit religious education. Embedded theology can be what we believed as children, or it may be the beliefs we currently hold that have been crafted through a lifetime of experiences that have impressed themselves upon our unconscious mind without disciplined reflection. If we imagine the theology that guides us throughout our lives as a growing tree, the embedded theology begins as a seed. It is the beliefs and assumptions that were passed on to us by our parents, planted in the fertile ground of our childhood or foundational church homes. In this environment, the seeds of our theology grow into roots. These roots ground us, but a tree cannot flourish if it doesn't grow past its roots. If we leave our embedded theology unexamined, our support system of theological roots can become theological baggage that weighs us down with its lack of intentional development. If we allow this to happen, the theologies that sprouted our faith can end up chocking it into rigid and shallow understandings.

Deliberative theology, on the other hand, is theology that we intentionally craft as we grow and mature spiritually. We create our deliberative theology through the active reflection on our embedded beliefs, along with continued study and learning. In forming our own deliberative theology, we take our embedded theologies to task based on our own lived experiences, understandings, and environments. This forces us to examine our assumptions, the things that we have taken for granted. We ask ourselves, "Do the things that I have been taught about God and about my faith align with what I see and hear and feel?" As we begin to explore our faith, learning to worship God through our questions, the deliberative practice creates the trunk of our theological tree. This intentional exercise allows us to move past the shallow foundation of our roots and allows us to flourish.

By intentionally developing our own theological perspective, we are forced to grapple with the complexities and messiness that embedded theology too often ignores. The deliberative process forces us to live our faith, to listen for the voices and experiences of the unheard. With time, dedication, and an open heart, we can grow a rich theological perspective that branches out, producing fruits of right and righteous belief and action.

Being Prophetic

Ethical prophecy is the telling of divine truth—that which discloses God's self—by means of unmasking the reality of the world's condition of suffering to the promised hope of God. This cry is a proclamation of truth. It is determining and then living out just and ethical ways. Pastors and other leaders often experience a sense of being called by God to this task of prophetic proclamation. On matters of justice, we feel the weight of the task and its burden of responsibility.

Prophetic responsibility mandates that Christian faith should dialogue and participate ethically within the public square. Prophetic responsibility embodies a radical love ethic. Thus, ethical prophecy is a pattern for reshaping authentic communities rooted in faith, particularly Christian faith traditions.[2]

---

2. Mary Alice Mulligan and Rufus Burrow Jr., *Daring to Speak in God's Name: Ethical Prophecy in Ministry* (Cleveland: Pilgrim Press 2002), 23.

Ultimately, individuals and communities are responsible for participating in the ongoing struggle for their liberation as well as the liberation and freeing of others.[3]

As leaders in ministry, we have the power to create change, but we must be willing to use our power and privilege to do so. We must acknowledge that even though it isn't our fault, it is still our fight. And as leaders, we must compel others to acknowledge this truth too.

In general, ministry is an ongoing struggle of the church to define and redefine its roles, theological positions, and practices. A prophetic understanding of ministry commits itself to fostering community. It empowers a community and its constituency to overcome their respective social, economic, political, and spiritual challenges. More importantly, it invites exploration and experimentation toward the development of new missional communities and leaders.

> *Ethical prophetic witness is the telling of divine truth by means of unmasking the reality of the world's condition of suffering, and pointing to the promised hope of God's infinite love, care, compassion, and justice.*

Ethical prophecy requires not only a sense of urgency but also sensitivity to the following considerations:

1. Oppressive conditions exist worldwide and demand an immediate response.

2. Concerns of God are matters of life and death.

---

3. See Martin Luther King Jr.'s ideas about power and liberation in Coretta Scott King, ed., *The Words of Martin Luther King, Jr.* (New York: New Market Press, 1983).

3. Solidarity is critical in the formation of the "new" humanity.

In that process of developing new missional communities and leaders, we ought to find ourselves asking questions such as the following: What is the will, the ways, and the word of God for such a time as this? How do we align ourselves with that? What does ethical prophetic witness look like in our own communities and congregations? Who has the "power"? What structures and systems do we need to address...and to what aim?

The Hard Truth

Often people ask, why do churches not participate in social justice? Why do persons not engage in service to others? In his book *Doing What's Right,* Tavis Smiley postulates the following as reasons why people do not engage in service: they don't know how; they're just too busy; they are disconnected; they fear the consequences of action; or they don't believe anything they do will result in change.[4]

The difficult truth is, we're not all that interested in being prophetic—because prophets have to figure out how to be present with people who don't want to hear their message. Jeremiah and Moses dealt with that reality constantly. "They won't listen!" they complained oft times to God. Walter Fluker reminds us, "When you stand at the centermost place of your convictions and dare to speak and act in public, expect to get creamed! The intersection is a dangerous territory."[5]

---

4. Tavis Smiley, *Doing What's Right: How to Fight for What You Believe—And Make a Difference* (New York: Anchor, 2009).

5. Walter Earl Fluker, *Ethical Leadership: The Quest for Character, Civility, and Community* (Minneapolis: Fortress Press, 2009), 72.

Regardless of the people's willingness to engage our messages, faith practitioners and change agents have to discern how best to lead and be present with their respective communities. We have to concern ourselves with people who are well intentioned or perfectly capable of helping—but who do not know how or, more likely, are not seriously committed to doing so. Even when folks say they are "on board," leaders still have to stand in the face of the system and keep face with everyone—on all sides of the community crisis.

In addition to my other responsibilities in Ferguson, I also instruct seminary students. The spring after Michael Brown's shooting, the grand jury's decision not to indict the police officer involved, and the ensuing unrest, I opened my class by asking my students to define *ethical prophetic witness.* Without exception, they responded, "Speaking truth to power." That's a fine answer, but it's incomplete.

"When do you get to do that?" I asked. The truth is, few, if any, of those students will get an interview on National Public Radio. Many were not serious about getting arrested, putting their bodies in physical danger, and risking their livelihood. It's not likely they'll see one hundred days of protest just outside their front door. And this is the real sticking point: most of these seminary students are probably going to serve as pastors in churches that are small and struggling, where the congregation is focused on a myriad of other concerns, and where race and injustice are nowhere near the top of the church's priority list. Their parishioners will probably, for the most part, be unconcerned about these issues and unlikely to actively support this work in any significant way. Perhaps this describes the scenario where you are serving now. It's a bleak picture, but we can lead it to change.

When we think of prophetic voice as only speaking truth to power, we ignore all of the other ways that we as believers and faith leaders can be prophetic. We can all be prophetic in our own contexts. It only takes a shift of focus, a willingness to learn and listen, and a certain level of comfort in being discomforted. The crises of the day are so great that complacency is no longer an option. The circumstances and conditions for which we live have reached a critical mass, and a radical response of love and change is required. I've included in this book contributions from friends and colleagues from a variety of professional backgrounds who provide prophetic voices in their own way and in their own contexts. These testimonies are meant to be examples to prompt your reflection about your particular place and space, where your voice is needed to pursue justice and bring God's kingdom into your community's lived reality.

Our Communities Are Trauma Patients

We need to begin to see our communities right now as trauma patients, as a hurt one lying on the mat. We are in a critical state. We must understand that the initial effort in trauma and in critical care situations is to bring some stability. Protests and street rallies express frustration, grief, a sense of insecurity and fear in the face of recurring practices and systems in which people feel susceptible to victimization.

A just society is to be judged by how well it treats the weakest, poorest, and most pained of its members.[6] The church specifically must remain answerable to a similar critique. Our current systems are malignant and myopic, able only to label or categorize, not grant genuine autonomy. They allow us, and sometimes even encourage us, to make caricatures of individuals based on assumptions, biases, and stereotypes, rather than celebrating our divinely given personhood.

---

6. Mulligan and Burrow, *Daring to Speak in God's Name: Ethical Prophecy in Ministry*, 37.

Our God is the God of shalom—the Hebrew word for peace. God is wholly concerned about humanity and all of creation. We faith leaders, too, should be concerned about humanity and creation's material and relational well-being. We should be concerned that all persons experience loving and just relationships. We should be concerned about and involved in ethical and moral considerations.

The very problem of antiquity is the same problem for the contemporary church. There is too much protecting of individual territory and structures of power. There is an excessive amount of interest in protecting a singular narrative or portion of history. There is too much emphasis placed on protection of one's piece of a pew, role in worship, and share of money. Unfortunately, there is not enough earnest practicing of peace, righteous action, or just relationship.

Jesus's life was purposed so that the perfect will of God would be achieved. Such is the design and disposition of our lives. That's why the mantra "It's not about me…it's not about we…It's about Thee" is powerful and prophetic. Christian leaders, we must strive to have our homes, workplaces, friendship circles, and communities of faith become caring places driven by God's purpose!

Chapter Two
EMPATHIC MODELS OF TRANSFORMATION

After a few days, Jesus went back to Capernaum, and people heard
that he was at home. So many gathered that there was no longer
space, not even near the door. Jesus was speaking the word to them.
Some people arrived, and four of them were bringing to him a man
who was paralyzed. They couldn't carry him through the crowd, so
they tore off part of the roof above where Jesus was. When they had
made an opening, they lowered the mat on which the paralyzed
man was lying. When Jesus saw their faith, he said to the paralytic,
"Child, your sins are forgiven!"

Some legal experts were sitting there, muttering among themselves,
"Why does he speak this way? He's insulting God. Only the one God
can forgive sins."

Jesus immediately recognized what they were discussing, and he said
to them, "Why do you fill your minds with these questions? Which
is easier—to say to a paralyzed person, 'Your sins are forgiven,' or
to say, 'Get up, take up your bed, and walk'? But so you will know
that the Human One has authority on the earth to forgive sins"—
he said to the man who was paralyzed, "Get up, take your mat,
and go home."

Jesus raised him up, and right away he picked up his mat and walked out in front of everybody. They were all amazed and praised God, saying, "We've never seen anything like this!"

—Mark 2:1-12

Ministry fails when it ignores the needs of individuals and communities that are most vulnerable and victimized in our society. Our faith teaches us that every person has intrinsic value and inalienable rights. Unfortunately, we live in a world in which it is acceptable to discount others' value and to disregard their rights. The inequalities and multidimensional oppression experienced by so many are social constructions fashioned out of historical precedent, systematic and institutional replication, and cultural perpetuation. The human instinct to thrive matched with the divine imperatives of love and hope demands a radical response on behalf of those whom society selectively has deemed as "less than." Prophetic leadership requires us to respond to our dehumanizing society, using our faith as an ethical lens that can help in responding to hurt "others'" experience with hope.

The Story of the Paralytic

"The paralytic" is all we know him by. Perhaps he had resigned himself to the understanding that he would not be healed today. Or maybe ever. He could not help himself, and so he lay there on his mat—likely defeated. Surely without hope.

But then four men came by. We don't get their names either; nor do we hear the conversation that happened among them. Did the paralytic cry out to them? Did the four men attempt to simply walk by, avoiding eye contact? Which one of the four men grabbed the shoulders of the others and turned them back to offer help? How did the man react, and how did he address his rescuers?

We don't know any of those details—because they aren't important. What is important to this story is that the four men stopped. They decided to take action. And they followed through. These first responders arrived on the scene of trauma, extended urgent care, and then set out to carry the hurt one to the One who could make him whole.

But then they encountered a significant challenge: they couldn't get to Jesus. They knew Jesus could help the paralyzed man, but the crowd was so thick they simply couldn't reach him. Perhaps one of the men caught another's eye, and without much more than a nod of their heads, their strategy solidified. They carried the man to the roof of the house—likely soliciting additional help along the way. They tore an opening in the roof and lowered the paralytic down before Jesus. The story records that Hope saw their faith and the paralytic's wholeness was restored.

The Role and Responsibility of the Church

The contemporary church needs to revisit this story. Those four men who chose to hold up their corner of the paralytic's mat couldn't get to Jesus—but not because of Jesus; it was the crowd that was keeping their brother from receiving help. In Mark's narrative about the paralytic, the house referenced is filled to capacity. It is standing room only with a line wrapped around the back. It would have been virtually impossible for the four assisting the hurt one to make their way to Jesus—the source of help and hope. The men in this story were creative and industrious in finding another means and a way. But not everyone is so tenacious.

I take pause whenever I read this portion of text. One can't help but wonder how many have a similar experience when encountering our churches. Do you ever view demonstrations and other acts of civil disobedience as result of persons' inability to aptly access hope for the hurt? Too many of us in the church—the very people whom Jesus has empowered to be hope and healing in the world—are standing in between Jesus and people in need. We have become so focused on what is happening inside our respective enclosures and systems that we fail to recognize and understand what is actually going on around us. What points of entry to our churches have now been closed or made difficult to access? Are we relying on those outside to remain persistent—to create a way in for themselves to be heard or helped—instead of extending hope from the inside?

In the narrative of the paralytic, we learn that when Jesus saw their faith—the four who brought their brother and lowered him through the roof—the man was healed. Christ saw himself in what they were doing. The power for us to heal or to offer hope resides in us and in the acts we present to Christ. In other words, we have to understand that Christ is not far off. He is God with us—Emmanuel. God is here. We have a responsibility—a shared work—to be part of the transformational experience. We have power that needs to be wielded for the greater good. Christ avails himself to us and we are invited to respond. To act.

Yet, we very often don't.

Our problem is that we are looking for some sort of formula to help us know what to do and when we should do it. There is no particular foolproof method or surefire set of strategies. The men who helped the paralytic were likely on their way to someplace else. But they stopped, picked up the hurt one, and took him to Jesus. Unfortunately, many folks today don't recognize our churches as the place of help and hope—the place to encounter Jesus. Too often, people in pain are sent home without experiencing the radical love of God.

Perhaps that's because we are not seeing them—the "other." We're trying too hard to discover ministry abroad, when all we really need to do is step out our own front door. If we are willing to truly see, we will immediately and, if we allow ourselves to, intimately recognize things that should grab our attention. In regard to race, our congregations must recognize that the divides and disconnects that come about because of privilege are problematic—because those are reflections of our failure to fully love one another. As disciples we are supposed to—ought to—love one another.[1] It's how people will know that we are followers of Christ—by our love. If we want to not only talk the talk but also walk the walk, this should be of great concern for the church.

However, historically, this simply hasn't been the case. People don't want to acknowledge that we have a historical imprint of violence and hatred, a consistent and systematic demeaning and devaluing of persons that spans long before our time. It is painful and difficult to admit that we benefit from and play a part in systems that cause and continue the oppression of others. These great systems have been memorialized and systematized through our institutions to the point that they have metaphorically and perhaps literally been embedded into our DNA. Our attitudes and our behaviors are natural—nearly instinctive—and they have a direct impact on culture. The truth is that the concerns in our communities are issues of humanity. In other words, simply because they disproportionately affect particular people, they affect all of us. As long as we remain naïve to that fact and refuse to look within ourselves as Christ's body and hold one another accountable, we will not be effective.

---

1. Privilege is power associated with social identification. We will further define and explore privilege later in this book.

Empathic Model of Transformation: Acknowledge, Affirm, Act

Our community and our world are hurting. This trauma necessitates that each of us grab a corner of the human fabric and cooperatively work to realize healing. Debilitated, despondent, and dispirited people and problems must be carried to points where health and wholeness can be restored. It's the church's responsibility to be among the first responders—not as Emergency Medical Technicians but, I propose, to offer Empathic Models of Transformation (EMT).

The basis of EMT is empathy—a "oneness" with others. In his work, Walter Fluker, Martin Luther King Jr. Professor of Ethical Leadership at the Boston University School of Theology, explains empathy as "capacity of the [ethical] leader to put him- or herself in the other's place.... Empathy is really about feelings, intelligent feelings being cultivated through practice."[2] Fluker says that empathy begins not with speaking but with listening. Howard Thurman characterized this as the "sound of the genuine."

I concur with Fluker and Howard. Listening to others' stories is a moral obligation.

How do we achieve that oneness of empathy? It is not an easy or quick accomplishment, like flipping on an empathy switch. And as life goes on, even faith leaders can become calloused, jaded, immune. Empathy is initiated through acknowledgment. *Acknowledgment* is acceptance of another's very existence—by truly seeing and listening to them. Too many of our tribe—our human tribe—are muted and invisible. Women, men, and children of diverse identities are rendered

---

2. Walter Fluker, in *Ethical Leadership: The Quest for Character, Civility, and Community*, discusses empathy as "capacity of the [ethical] leader to put him- or herself in the other's place." He describes the practice as being emotive, yet intelligent feelings being cultivated through practice. He goes on further to detail empathy as vulnerability and risk in the face of the other because as you see her (his) face, she (he) can also see yours.

silent and out of sight of society, the paralysis of their lives unexamined or unaddressed. In order to become EMTs, we must acknowledge difference. We must be aware of our own social location and the ways in which we benefit from systems of oppression. While acknowledgment is fundamentally about the other, it requires us to also learn more about ourselves and our relationship to the issues of the day. There are many things that are not right at the intersections of our lives. Whether geopolitical, social, or economic, acknowledgment is recognizing the moral and ethical inequities that abound and seeking to rectify them by intellectual and spiritual means.

Once we have acknowledged someone's humanity, we can move on to affirmation—respecting their humanity. Hear this: *affirmation* is neither an act of complicity nor condemnation. Affirming someone's experience—respecting their humanity in their own experience—does not mean you approve their ideology or behavior. We can love people without agreeing with them. That bears repeating: we can love people without agreeing with them. In the words of Howard Thurman, "Hatred does not empower, it decays. *Only through self-love and love for one another can God's justice prevail.*"[3] In short, affirmation is a willingness to emphasize our interdependence and commonality over our differences.

Lastly, living out Empathic Models of Transformation requires us to act. The imperative is to do something—to dare enough to care. That "something" will be different in every context, because the challenges are unique in each community. But ultimately the principle is the same: Caring is being present with each other. Caring is not grounded in the strong over the weak; the powerful leaning toward, or over, the powerless; or the haves merely aiding have-nots. Acts of caring occur when we enter into another's pain. Caring is shared presence, mutual experiences, and connected concerns.

---

3. Howard Thurman, *Jesus and the Disinherited* (Boston: Beacon Press, 1996).

From One Corner
St. Stephens and The Vine, Ferguson, Missouri
by Rev. Steve Lawler

Each of us has our own version of this story. Here is mine.

Michael Brown was killed on a Saturday. The news of the shooting was slow to come out. The St. Louis Post Dispatch site had a story up that evening. There were a couple of tweets and a few mentions on Facebook. On the next day, Sunday, things began to change. As I was having lunch with my son, I tried to imagine what Michael Brown's parents must be feeling. I tried to imagine what I would feel if my son was killed. Midway through lunch, my phone started buzzing. One text told me that a time of prayer in front of the police station had turned into a protest. Another from a mother of a son in his early twenties told me that things were accelerating. She was scared. I headed to the police station. Ferguson's shift from "Tree City USA," small-town Americana, to birthplace of the new civil rights movement was underway.

People hit the streets on Sunday night. West Florissant near where Darren Wilson shot Michael Brown began to fill with protesters. Policing became more aggressive, and by the end of the evening a QuikTrip was set on fire. After spending some of the evening out in Ferguson, I went home. I stayed up late following things as Twitter kicked in and local news coverage grew. Monday there were more people protesting and a now-militarized police presence. On Tuesday I was on the news talking about stores being closed and our food pantry being empty. That same night my son was hit by a rubber bullet. There was no place to go but forward.

Acknowledge

These early days were full of moments that prompted and in fact required acknowledgment, the first of the steps in what F. Willis Johnson identifies in the Empathic Models of Transformation (EMTs). Acknowledging that something is less than what is just, right, and loving is the beginning of our participation in God's holy work. It is opening our eyes to see what is happening in our midst. As things escalated in Ferguson I had to begin to acknowledge that the comfortable and safe places I traveled were places of privilege. I also had to acknowledge that things were difficult in the now with neighborhoods being locked down and people running out of food. In this moment, moving from acknowledgment to affirmation of the dignity of the many who were locked down and locked out of their neighborhoods propelled me forward. The uncomfortable place that was opening up became the faithful place to be.

Affirm

The interview about the food pantry ran at 6 p.m. At 7 the first car rolled onto the parking lot filled with food for the pantry. Travel in and out of the neighborhoods was getting harder and harder. It was impossible to ignore the reality of people's pain, their actual hunger. We didn't realize or articulate it at the time, but this was a chance for us to listen, to see, to be present with people in the midst of their pain.

A cadre was forming. People began to show up at the Parish Hall to sort, bag, and deliver food. We chilled bottled water for the people out on those 90° days and nights. There were sandwich lines to feed protesters. From early morning until late at night we gathered and delivered food and water. In conversations during those hours we began to realize how little we understood about the challenges of facing violence. We talked about food deserts and the limits of public transportation. The way policing is used against people. The lack of jobs.

Act

Relationships—and opportunities to act—grew with the flow of food. For years at St. Stephens we had talked about being a place of hospitality. Now we were getting to practice hospitality at light speed and in battlefield conditions: honoring those who protested, welcoming those who donated and helped, and gratefully accepting the sharing of food and time with people whose neighborhoods were filled with the press, protesters, and police. We found ourselves responding by our actions to a covenantal question from the Book of Common Prayer, "Will you strive for justice and peace among all people, and respect the dignity of every human being?"

In those early days our actions focused on hospitality. But, as a deacon said to me at one point, "A bag of food isn't enough." Other things began to happen. People who had worked side by side delivering food attended justice department meetings together and became involved with the police department's efforts to reform, which are just now beginning. As protests continued the relational space grew to include people who came to Ferguson to provide medical assistance, legal counsel, trauma support, and activities for kids since the schools were closed. Some of the cadre worked tirelessly to elect new city council members. All sorts of connections and relationships were formed. Peoples' initial response continues to ripple through Ferguson.

In this cycle of acknowledging/affirming/acting, the action part became the hardest step. I was increasingly in situations where white people had questions, made statements, and otherwise showed up with perceptions that I felt I needed to engage. I began to have the difficult conversations that are so much a part of holding up one's corner. Two of these conversations happened with some regularity. I call the first one the "Why are they rioting?" conversation. The second one, "I am not racist...."

The first conversation starts in various ways but ends up collapsing the complexity and power of what has been happening in Ferguson and countless other places into narratives of lawlessness. Version include, "Why don't they vote and change things that way?" The common theme: the black are not doing what the white think is best. These are tough conversations to have. Trying to communicate the deep frustration and inspired passion of those who lead this new movement is tricky. Defensiveness shows up. Reactivity does too. The term *white fragility* was new to me. Its presence became increasingly clear. So my work now is, in part, simply being a white guy with others who are white having essential conversations about whiteness, privilege, and racial and economic justice.

The second conversation symbolizes how many of us keep from acknowledging the system that works for us. I have said to myself and heard others say, "I am not racist." But in fact I am racist. I benefit from racial injustice. I have a hard time seeing beyond color. Many of my assumptions, thoughts, and reactions come from living my entire life within the systems that favor my whiteness, where I do not experience the violence and oppression women and men of color face constantly.

Acknowledging these biases and benefits is a constant part of holding up my corner. Affirming the others' real experiences of injustice and inequity is a constant process of conversion. And the slow daily work of taking actions that disrupt my own narratives and those of other white people is neither valorous nor unique. It is how we live into the Beloved Community. My aim is to acknowledge my embeddedness in a racist system, to affirm that others are discovering and challenging their own "whiteness," and to engage clearly and compassionately with other white people in constructive and transformative conversations. All of this leads to right actions and gospel relationships.

Here's what being an EMT means to me:

Acknowledge something is wrong or unjust.

Affirm the sacredness of persons, the reality of other people's experience, and the validity of their pain.

Act to do something, starting from wherever you are, with whatever you have, for betterment to come.

And:

Open our eyes to the realities in our community—where God's reign and kingdom is not yet overcoming selfishness, injustice, inequality, or the forces of evil.

Own the calling and responsibility we have as Christians, and advocate hope for God's kingdom in our particular community.

Organize interventions and activate mission teams to address the specific injustices in our particular community.

Part Two
BEING EMT'S

Chapter Three
ACKNOWLEDGE

In order to do justice, we must first acknowledge that there are things in our world and in our community that are not right. There are things we do that are simply not right. People we love and respect do things that are simply not right. Public figures—people whom we look up to—do things that are simply not right. Institutions that we believe in and love do things that are simply not right.

These things are not only not right, they are not righteous. They are not in alignment with the will and words and ways of God. We have taken our first step toward justice when we begin to acknowledge not only that there is difference in the world, but that our approach and reaction to these differences fails to meet our divine call toward love. This step is very small and may seem incremental, but we must be intentional about it. We must pause and do this step with full consciousness, instead of rushing past what may seem to be an insignificant point.

We must acknowledge that it's not right that as soon as we exit the highway, someone is standing in the heat in need of something to eat. It's not right that there's an imbalance of purpose and power, not just politically, but also in other realms of leadership. General care in the world is lacking. Our failure to address unjust and inequitable treatment of persons in our local communities and world has produced some deadly results. Our failure to honor and follow God's command-ments, precepts, and principles in our individual and corporate lives has led, in many instances, to our deathly and dying state.

How We Got Here

Historically, people have been categorized principally around color, and then whatever else is convenient or clearly distinguishable followed. This is what we mean when we identify race as a "social construct." We are divided by race because race has historically been used to put people in categories that prevent collaboration and support existing power structures. Our skin tones may differ outside of societal influ-ence, but individuals and societies across history have constructed our definitions of race and racial categories through placing value systems on these biological differences. The consequence of the takeover and inquisition between Europe and Africa is ultimately a caste system—a social construct of division and inequity that has been built largely around distinctions in skin tone. Since that time, people of European descent have been able to control the identification and manipulation of those variables, which gave them an advantage. They were able to start the race a little bit faster and farther ahead than others. They had a head start at exercising and leveraging their dominance by accumu-lating wealth through demeaning and oppressive means. Any time you have the ability or capacity to leverage self, wealth, or some semblance of insight or wisdom over another, to their demise or to their disadvan-tage, that is exercising privilege.

Our cultures and systems have the historical imprint of violence, hatred, and devaluing of persons. These patterns have been memorial-ized and systematized and institutionalized to the point that they are now embedded in us, culturally coded into our DNA. Our attitudes, assumptions, and behaviors related to "difference" are almost so instinctive and natural that we fail to recognize them or understand their true impact. We are mostly unaware, because these responses are so ingrained. This entrenched nature of systems makes creating change difficult. Often times, it is harder to change internalized structures than external systems. You can't legislate love. No judge or jury can pass a sentence that will render divine justice.

Intersectionality

Our culture and society forces all of us into boxes, often times binary boxes that erase the reality of other identities. You are black or white. You are male or female. You are able or disabled. Without intentional reflection or personal experience to the contrary, it is easy for us to believe that these boxes are real and definitive. However, the reality is that each and every one of us falls into a myriad of categories. For instance, I am black and I am male and I have a terminal degree. I exist at the intersection of these identities and many more; I am many things at once. So, too, is everyone that I come into contact with—including you. We all fall into many categories and are assigned, or self-select, many identities. We must resist the urge to collapse conversations about difference into conversations about one kind of identity. I cannot talk about black liberation without noting the difference of experience and needs of black women. Even further, I cannot speak of the liberation of black women without asking how LGBTQ women experience racism in a way that differs from straight women. I cannot address issues of othering without noticing that white folks with disabilities experience their whiteness differently than able-bodied individuals.

Our world is hurting. There are so many individuals, so many places, so many communities who are hurting. We experience different struggles. We face different structural oppressions. Dominant culture reacts to us in different ways. Ultimately, though, the experience of being "othered" is shared. At many points this book will speak specifically about racial injustice and racial difference. However, at its core, this is a book about difference and othering. All "others" need to be acknowledged and affirmed. In order to pursue justice, we must hear the hollering not only of the racial other but of all individuals who are "othered" and harmed by our society. Hearing the hollering of "others" calls us to authentically hear the hollering of one another.

Injustice and Inequality Are Sin

The concept of sin is typically viewed as solely religious. However, this tendency to connect sin with personal piety has atrophied the power of thinking about sin. Truthfully, much of what is wrong in our communities, world, and personal spaces is the result of sin. Sin is anything that distances us from God. It is that which distracts or discourages individuals from sensing or experiencing the love of God. Sin is anything that encroaches upon, impedes, or ignores another's inalienable rights and nature to be not only free but also whole and alive. Injustice and inequalities of any make or model are *sin*. What also needs to be said and understood is that all of us are sinners, in some minuscule or massively oppressive way. That is why the biblical record states that all have sinned and fallen short of the glory, or divine expectations, of God.

Neither creation nor the created endure negative or consequential response for being wrong. Rather, we experience consequences in doing wrong or bringing about wrongness. This wrongness is in contrast to God's "ought-ness."

This idea of wrongness and ought-ness of God is the source of great historical debate, institutional division, and cultural and civil discord. It is a theological question that challenges biblical interpretations, doctrinal stances, denominational, human, and socially contrived standards and norms. We are not punished "for" our sins, but "by" our sins. God does not dole out punitive punishments; rather, we are punished by our sin through direct consequences. We do not experience commensurate bad, hurtful, inhumane, or catastrophic consequences for our sins, because neither God nor the universe is merely retaliatory. Our sin distances us from God, and we suffer because of this distance. All things spiritual play out in real time. All actions have a cause and effect, and we have to live with the effects that sin creates on our lives. If we fail to love our neighbor, we have to live with the distance we've created between ourselves and God and the distance between ourselves and our neighbors. We have to live with the tension that we have inserted into our own community.

The ways we talk about sin need to reflect the lived realities of our world. Personal sin is important to discuss, but we must also pay attention to the ways in which we sin against others in the communal sphere. Our current capitalist system is neither right nor righteous. This is not due to the sin of one individual, but rather it is a collective sin. We all sin together in our complicity with and willful ignorance of oppressive systems. Personal sin may rarely lead to hunger, but the selfish way an individual functions and lives—which is multiplied many times in the collective of United States citizens as a whole—creates hunger, and therefore is sinful. Ignorance grants no immunity from the law, and neither does it grant immunity from our divine responsibility to our neighbor.

The Problem with Privilege

The term *privilege* has been thrown around a lot lately. It has become a buzzword or a talking point for the floating heads on our television. It is a term that is used often, but sparsely defined. It is a word that can turn a friendly conversation into a political debate in a matter of seconds. Despite its current status as a "controversial" term, the concept behind privilege really isn't very complicated. Privilege is any advantage or lack of disadvantage that any person or group of persons receive. White folks experience privilege when they are not stopped by the police because of their skin tone. Men experience privilege when they can hold leadership positions without being seen as bossy or manipulative. Straight folks experience privilege when they walk down the street holding hands with a romantic partner without fear of harassment or threat of violence. Affluent folks experience privilege when they go to their fridge and find a variety of food choices.

It is critical to acknowledge that we all enjoy certain privileges, and we have to lead our congregations to understand that as well. They may not like it, but important lessons are rarely comfortable. Keep in mind, we don't have to make everything about "wrong" and "right." Neither privilege nor power is inherently good or bad. Values cannot be attributed to our privileged status, but rather in how we wield this privilege. Privilege is what it is, and we all have it. We all have it. You were able to buy this book. You're able to read it. We're able to share it through regular access to technological tools. If you and I wield that privilege—that power—to the demise and detriment of others, that's where we've wronged, even if the harm caused was unintentional.

Some of you might be thinking, "Okay, I have privilege, but I am not a racist!" It's probably true that no one has actually ever called you a racist. But the concept of privilege triggers defensive responses in many of us. When you recognize and consider your own privilege, does it raise your blood pressure just a little? Why is that? Why do you feel that way? How does the term *privilege* affect you, and what's at the root of your response? How is it touching you? You don't want to be called racist. What does that mean to you—what would it mean to you to be called racist? What responses and feelings are you internalizing?

Keep in mind: acknowledging is not the same as accepting blame. Just because you recognize your own advantages and you acknowledge the disadvantages of others, doesn't mean that the injustice is your fault.

As you begin to absorb the reality of privilege, also keep in mind that we are not out to shame folk; we are out to same folk. This is not encouragement to go out and flog ourselves for our privilege; instead the recommendation is that we acknowledge we have "it," and then determine how we can use "it" to uplift one another, rather than destroy.

The ways in which the apostle Paul dealt with his privilege illustrate this idea perfectly. He was educated—the Rhodes Scholar of antiquity. There's no question that he was privileged in that way and in many others. And yet, at places where it made sense, where it was appropriate and necessary, Paul leveraged his privilege. He did so not for his benefit, but to gain access to the systems misappropriating power, so he could expose and challenge them.

But he also was willing to release his privilege. He said, "I can become anything. Whatever I need to be, wherever I need to be to meet people where they are, I'm going to do that." Moreover, there were times he could have spoken up and kept himself out of harm's way, kept himself from being wrongly profiled and confronted by police, but he did not. He chose to be in solidarity with the people, because he was one of them. In our Christian communities, we need to start saying that "whatever it is that makes us different, we have one Lord, one faith, and one baptism, and we are inextricably, and unexplainably at times, connected. There is no Jew or Gentile. We are the same."

In order to create change, we must first do the hard work of acknowledging the injustices present across the world, our church, and our local communities, as well as our own privilege. Faithful people can no longer afford not to look away from the racial disparity, violence, and injustice that fill our twenty-four-hour news cycles. Generations of hurt, distrust, and myopia have created a society that divides and categorizes according to perceived differences—differences that hold no meaning in God's kingdom. Stereotypes and bias, both implicit and explicit, create a blindness that inhibits our unity within community.

Ultimately, we must boldly invite God into this place of blindness to heal the hurt at the core of our unstable societies and clashing cultures. This must be an intentional invitation to healing through prayer and reconciliation with justice.

Savior Mentality

For those of us who hold positions of privilege, it is vital to recognize that vulnerable and victimized classes, particularly people of color, have been doing the heavy lifting of explaining, facilitating, and teaching for far too long. We can no longer make it incumbent upon the hurt to source out their own healing. We cannot expect the black individuals in our circles, offices, or classes to speak for all people of color or to be responsible for our education on matters of race. We cannot claim to stand in solidarity with communities where we have not built any relationships. We cannot expect those who experience oppression to explain systems of oppression to us. We cannot sign up to help an after-school program in someone else's neighborhood, in a different culture context, and then complain when there aren't organized tasks for us to do. We can't claim to be helping others if we are requiring more effort and resource from them in our helping.

At Trinity United Church of Christ in Chicago there is a beautiful oil painting that hangs in the vestibule. A placard underneath the painting reads "We Are Unashamedly Black and Unapologetically Christian." The painting, the slogan, and their prominent placement in the church indicate that this church has boldly confronted one of the four major challenges confronting the church today: how to be authentically black and authentically Christian at the same time. If we as Christians ignore racial and culture differences, we are failing our brothers and sisters in Christ. If we are not sensitive to difference in perspective, experience, and need, we are not engaging "others" authentically.

Rather than approaching communities in need and asking "how can I help?" individuals of privilege should reflect on the ways in which they are able and willing to help and offer specific assistance as discerned and advised by their beneficiaries. Our work with communities that differ from our own should focus on solidarity and mutual development and support, rather than a notion that "I" can serve (or save) "you." We must shift our practices of charity toward the creation of relationships that breed solidarity. We must push ourselves and hold ourselves accountable, rather than expecting others to do that work for us. We cannot expect the "other" to show us the way. We have to be willing to use our own position and power to educate and find a way ourselves.

Your Story, Your Biases

When I first started my doctorate work, my advisor shared this story with me:

Every night at bedtime, a man read aloud the same book to his son. In this story, a hunter tracks a lion through the jungle, carefully waiting until the moment is right before ultimately capturing his dangerous foe. One night, the little boy asked his father why the lion always had to be captured in the end of the story. Surprised, the man answered, "Because the hunter wrote the story."

The stories we have and the stories we hear matter. In fact, stories have built the institutions that shape us. Racism, homophobia, sexism, and all of the other -isms are a part of the cultural fabric that informs us at every turn. It is like the water we swim in—we may not be able to see it, but it is all around, influencing our every thought and action. This reality of culture gives us all unconscious biases—unconscious inclinations or preferences that interfere with impartial judgment. Unconscious bias is not hatred; it is our unknown and unintentional preferences and includes all of the ways that oppressive structures have entered into our minds. The privileges we have make us blind to our biases, because privilege often keeps us from noticing inequality.[1]

For example, a white woman may have an unconscious bias that causes her to hold her purse more tightly if she walks past a black man at night. She may not even be aware of this change in posture. Her actions are influenced by the images of black men as criminals that fill our TVs and computer screens, rather than conscious thought. This woman may believe that white and black men are treated the same by criminal justice officials and organizations, and yet her own behavior toward these two groups is different. Her privilege and lack of experience with the ways that our society seeks to criminalize and control black bodies have blinded her to the dissimilarity in lived experiences.

---

1. To learn more about unconscious or implicit bias or to take a test to determine your own unconscious bias and contribute to the academic study of bias, visit the Project Implicit site at https://implicit.harvard.edu/implicit/takeatest.html.

These unconscious biases can only be confronted through a process of self-reflection and a willingness to learn from the experiences and stories of others. Unfortunately, this self-reflection doesn't always happen naturally. When was the last time you were intentional about reflecting on the things that create your ideas and beliefs around issues of difference, such as race? When was the last time you picked up a mirror to figure out what has affected your understandings and assumptions on race? Each of us must come to understand our own story and social location to determine our frame of reference and to better understand our own perspectives. According to Mulligan and Burrow, this concept of "acknowledging" requires "remembering that where one stands socially, economically, and politically really does affect what one sees and what one is blind to in church and society. A person's perspective also has much to do with how he responds to what is seen."[2] At the Center for Social Empowerment, we refer to this reflection on our own societal placement as our *racial autobiography*. It is a purposeful reflection on our own social location that allows us to better understand our own experiences, and opens us to the differences in the experiences of others.

Our lives are fundamentally a patchwork of stories and experiences informed by our social, economic, and political location. We have been formed throughout our lifetimes by our loved ones, our schools, our churches, our friends, the media we consume, traumatic and empowering experiences, along with so much more. We often glide through life moving from one experience to the next without much reflection, paying more attention to the overarching plot of our lives: our next job, our next birthday, getting through school, getting our kids to graduation day. True acknowledgment requires more of us. It requires us to think about how we have come to understand and experience difference over the course of our lives. It is thinking about the ways that our

---

2. Mary Alice Mulligan and Rufus Burrow Jr., *Daring to Speak in God's Name: Ethical Prophecy in Ministry* (Cleveland: Pilgrim Press 2002), 23.

grandparents informed our views on sexuality. It is thinking about the first time we experienced or witnessed racial discrimination. It is thinking about how transgendered characters are portrayed in the television shows we watch.

Our own story is most likely not a clear line from birth to the present. It is a bumpy road with many twists and turns, moments of confusion, and moments of breakthrough. Our views and opinions evolve and change—sometimes due to our own experiences and sometimes through learning from the experiences of others. Ultimately, coming to understand our own stories prepares us to authentically encounter the other. When we sort through our own history, we realize the particularity of experience that has created us. We begin to understand how we have come to be the person we are, which sheds a brighter light on who that person really is. Most importantly, reflecting on and figuring out our own stories prepares us to share and, in turn, to receive the stories of others.

The Other's Story, Their Language

In 2016, my work led me to the Seattle headquarters of my favorite corporate coffee shop. A colleague and I were joking about something and the barista took notice and joined our conversation. The barista was friendly, funny, and cheerful, everything you'd want from your server in a coffee shop. However, in the course of this exchange I began to feel a little off balance. I realized that the person standing behind the counter was transgender—their gender presentation did not meet my expectations. I found myself wondering, *What is going on here? Is the person standing in front of me a man or a woman? How am I supposed to talk to this person? What words or pronouns am I supposed to use?*

Finally, I understood that the answers to these questions did not matter. I asked the barista for their name.[3]

"I'm Shay."

"Thank you, Shay, it was nice to meet you." Rather than defining Shay based on my own biases and understanding, I allowed Shay to name and define their-self.

We all have an impulse to size people up and put them into categories. As soon as we meet someone new, our brain automatically goes into overdrive collecting information in order to place the other into boxes: man or woman; black, white, or brown; straight or gay; transgender or cisgender. This is not a bad thing; it is simply how our brains evolved and how our culture developed. The challenge lies in recognizing the ways we categorize people and opening ourselves up to the reality that our assumptions and automatic understanding may be incorrect, and in some ways, they may be unintentionally harmful or painful for the "other."

My conditioning and cultural competence does not take precedent over the dignity of the other. I was raised to say "yes sir" and "yes ma'am." I've been well educated, and I pay attention to the trends and normative behaviors in society. My religious tradition embraced the respectful identification of others through the endearing terms "brother" or "sister." I aim to be careful about the way I speak to people in general, to be sensitive to their feelings and circumstances. Pastors are trained to be polite. These practices are good and well intentioned when used appropriately, but this conditioned etiquette should not be idolized to the point that it becomes more important than the experience, emotional well-being, or identity of another.

---

3. The pronouns "they," "them," and "their-self" are used in identifying people who are gender-queer or gender nonconforming. I use "they" and "their-self" to refer to Shay because I do not know how they identify on the gender spectrum and wish to respect their ability to self-identify.

My need to honor the tradition of respect that I have been taught, my need to honor my upbringing and religious beliefs in all contexts, is an exertion of privilege. It may appease me, but it is not honoring the "other." It is our instinct in culturally tense situations to pour our effort and energy into preserving our own credibility. We also work hard not to look like fools or to cause offense. When I cling so tightly to my polite pastor persona, I am more concerned about myself than the "other." We must free ourselves from this trap. Honoring the "other" requires individuals to acknowledge persons in the manner in which they identify and define themselves. It requires you and me to abandon honorifics, and, often, to ask for preferred terms if the gendered language used does not fit into another's self-identification. It requires us to prioritize the feelings and experience of the other over our own.

The same principle for using language holds true for other kinds of "others." What would happen if, when you encounter a person who is somehow "other" to you, you were to lay aside your own conditioned etiquette and ask, "What do you want to be called?" or "How do you identify yourself?" or simply, "What's your name?" and leave it at that, letting the other person take the lead, letting the conversation go from there, centered on the other? What if, when you find yourself struggling with language, unsure of the "right" words to use so as not to offend or look foolish, you *ask the other* to guide you? What if you poured your energy into listening to that other person, rather than working so hard to find and correctly name the proper category for that person?

The Bible does not simply assign roles. The Bible message and model assigns responsibility. Everyone is covered by the canopy of God's love and grace, and we are also meant to *participate* in the covering. We each have a responsibility to one another as fellow humans. Humanity, like Jesus, is the *imago dei*, or image of God. The *imago dei* is what all persons irrespective of race, creed, gender, and socioeconomic status are and ought to be. The spirit of God resides inside each of us. Our lives are a daily struggle to let this divine light shine through the sins of selfishness and injustice.

Likewise, we have a responsibility to continually strive to recognize and respect the face of God that resides within each and every person with whom we interact. Everyone has a divine entitlement to respect and dignity, even individuals and communities that we do not agree with or understand. We must always push ourselves to remember that when we look into the face of the "other," we are looking at the spirit of God within them that mirrors the spirit of God within us, erasing the space between us and them. That is what acknowledgment is all about. When encountering the "other," we must focus not on our many differences, but rather, on our shared sacred identity as God's creation and our shared responsibility to care for one another.

Far too often, issues of difference are muted in our society. We go to great lengths to avoid talking about difference, especially race, by using coded language. Instead of saying "black," we talk about urban populations or use words like "thug." We implicitly identify and dance around difference, but we don't really engage with it. Acknowledgment requires us to not only identify but also genuinely engage in difference. It requires us to be attentive to our own stories as well as the stories of those who are somehow "other" to us. We have to force ourselves to begin to see those structures and systems in society that benefit some and hurt others. We must begin to explore how we contribute to and benefit from these systems. We have to be willing to hear the stories of those who are hurt by the practices and institutions in which we participate. Acknowledgment is the purposeful alertness to difference in experience, story, and identity.

Reflection Questions

1. How has your life been shaped by your race? Your gender? Your socio-economic class?

2. How have your attitudes about race and toward persons of other races/genders/classes/sexual orientations been shaped by your home, church, school, and work environments?

3. Have you experienced or witnessed privilege in your life? When did you first become aware of this privilege?

4. Have you experienced or witnessed discrimination in your life? When did you first become aware of this discrimination?

5. Where in your community do you see racial prejudice, entrenched poverty and exploitation, segregation, dwindling educational and employment opportunities, symptoms of failing social structures, and so forth?

From One Corner
Authentic Engagement from the Inside Out
Heidi J. Kim

Heidi J. Kim is the missioner for racial reconciliation for the Episcopal Church, responsible for facilitating the establishment and growth of networks in the church that confront structural issues of racism in society and the church. Her approach to the work of reconciliation is grounded in her commitments to lifelong spiritual formation, and deep listening to our shared stories of embracing the diversity that comprises the community of Christ.

In traveling across the country for the Episcopal Church as the missioner for racial reconciliation, Heidi has discovered that most US citizens engage in mission and service in search of administering help instead of coming in search of sharing experiences and learning. They want to help, not *be* helped, which leads to these experiences remaining one-sided—hence the efforts around resolving injustice are always viewed as the thing that other people *go and do*, taking over, over there and elsewhere. Far too often, persons of privilege or who experience life at the center see injustice as another's fault and responsibility. As Heidi says, "People make systematic and racial justice exotic...pointing to others' faults, confronting or opposing systems that wrong without being personally confronted themselves." Persons whose lives are experienced at the center, not on the margins, are thus afforded the opportunity to view injustice from afar. There is an important if subtle difference between this opposition from afar and the active, personal

43

engagement of privileged people with others, sharing their stories, understanding their experiences, and seeing them as fellow members of God's global family. Heidi doesn't let us privileged ones off the hook.

Far too often, our conversations around racial injustice are detached exercises instead of vulnerable conversations that require us to be authentic. Rather than engaging in this conversation from a bird's-eye view, Heidi encourages Episcopal congregants to engage in their own experiences and the experiences of others. Heidi calls this authentic sharing "the sound of the genuine." If we are willing to take the risk and open ourselves to our inner voice and the voices of those around us in all of their messiness, joy, and pain, we can begin to create authentic relationships and learning experiences that will propel us toward finding a form of action that will catalyze needed change.

In order to really do the work that is necessary to transform systems of injustice, Heidi focuses on the truth that everybody can enact justice from their own place or perspective if we would only open ourselves up to the stories around us. People often think that there is only one way to do justice; instead of starting with their respective gifts and skills and following their own call or vocation, they look to other people or to justice work made credible by people getting arrested, protesting in the streets, and so on. But when people listen to their own stories and the sound of the genuine in themselves, they can begin to engage in racial justice work in truly meaningful and transformative ways.

- A teacher who is passionate about reading can engage in justice work by including diverse literature in the classroom and facilitating classroom conversation that points students toward justice.

- A successful business person who is passionate about numbers may donate time to a local nonprofit that helps community members start new business ventures
- Folks who love to socialize and spend time with others can organize informal exchanges in common places like coffee shops or local pubs as simple means for telling and hearing stories.

We all must determine how our greatest talents and passions can be leveraged to create justice.

Chapter Four
AFFIRM

Upon the suggestion of a dear friend, I attended a discussion about engaging in and nurturing difficult conversations around the issue of race. As I sat in a room of more than two hundred people, where I was one of only a few black people in attendance, I pondered my situation. I questioned neither the content nor the metadata of the authors. Yet I was fixated on dissecting their choices in the practice of conversation. I wondered how you engage and nurture good conversations around difficult issues like race when key stakeholders of the subject matter, namely people of color, are visibly absent even if respectfully considered?

Immediately I began thinking, how do we have good conversation for the good of all? More importantly, how were we having a conversation for the good of all when there wasn't an ethnically or culturally diverse offering in the room? Where were the generational "others" in a room full of Generation X and hip Baby Boomers? Was this a safe space for LGBTQ persons to name and express their authentic selves? Was the wide spectrum of economic, political, and social pluralism represented fully enough to truly engage and nurture "good conversation"? How far could this rather homogenous gathering go toward a broader, deeper understanding of the unrepresented "others"?

The Beautiful Church

In antiquity, and still today, there exist places of worship that are aesthetically beautiful but spiritually barren. There are centers of faith in cities throughout this country and around the world that are beautiful places, but where ugly religion is practiced. When churches seek to protect riches over righteousness—that's some ugly stuff. When church constitutions and people contradict God's covenant; using politics to paralyze the pastor and make puppets out of prophets; placing tradition above the word of God—that's some ugly stuff. So how do we create and nourish spaces that are beautiful *and* houses of beautiful communion? Our beautiful churches should be centers of right relationship. Right relationship has constructive power; it must be encouraged in our church spaces and in our church communities.

There is a distinct and divinely defined difference between religion and relationship. Relationship is shared intimacy. Relationship is common and consistent communication. Relationship requires surrendering the self, submitting to another, sacrifice and service. The three major religions of the world—Islam, Judaism, and Christianity—honor relationship with God and one another over religion or religious dogma and tradition. Each of these faith movements' respective practices, symbols, and creeds endeavors to point not to self but toward God. The good news for you and me is that a beautiful place can produce a bountiful blessed reality if and when its members seek to align in right relationship with God. Every mosque, temple, and church is empowered to exercise righteous authority, extend a right hand of fellowship, and escort persons to a reverent and relevant space where those relationships can begin and blossom.

In order to exercise righteous authority, we have to believe that change is possible and promised in the lives of all. We have to activate and employ our faith. We have to believe in the possibility of relationship before we ever see it.

Before an architect ever builds a building, she conceptualizes it in her mind's eye. Architects further visualize and translate the idea to paper. All this happens before anything is ever built. Even before ground is broken, architects and contractors put up signs to say, "Here marks the spot where something that was imagined will become."

People will go broke—in money and energy—trying to build a beautiful place, but what would it look like to put the same resources into building right relationships?

The gift of relationship with God includes the relational ties that bind us to one another. If we practice faith and humility in our spiritual lives, we will encounter the opportunity to extend a right hand of fellowship and build up the church. When was the last time you reached out and touched someone? When was the last time you called someone not to gossip, but to see how they were doing and to pray with them? When was the last time you touched your spouse or children in a healthy, respectful, loving, or intimate way? When was the last time you shook hands with a stranger? Remember, there is power in a touch. As people of faith we are instructed to extend a lifeline to those who are drowning in *who they are presently* while trying to reach the shores of who they ought to be. We are also called to allow other peoples' stories and experiences to be our lifeline, to be the hand that pulls us into our "ought-ness."

The result of a beautiful relationship with God is that you and I can escort someone who was or is broken, bruised, battered, and needy to a reverent space. That reverent space can be a mosque, temple, church, or other sacred place. But the power residing in such places is our presence, our solidarity with the suffering. We have the gift from God to speak change into one another's life. We all have the power to heal, transform, revive, deliver, and restore one another's life. That is beauty. And people want to follow that which is beautiful.

When we encourage another's faith they will follow. When we enrich someone's life they will follow. When we empower another's spirit they will follow. We have the opportunity to lead people to live differently, to be more of who they ought to be! Let our mosques, temples, and churches be more than beautiful buildings. Let us also become beautiful people sharing in beautiful relationship.

Right Relationship: Unity amid Difference

Right relationship requires us to respect the differences between us, out of respect for our inherent unity. Martin Luther King Jr. wrote in his "Letter from a Birmingham Jail": "In a real sense all life is interrelated. All men are caught in an inescapable network of mutuality, tied in a single garment of destiny."[1]

This theme of oneness, of unity, is also found throughout scripture. Eugene Peterson translates the fourth chapter of Ephesians:

> You were all called to travel on the same road and in the same direction, so stay together, both outwardly and inwardly. You have one Master, one faith, one baptism, one God and Father of all, who rules over all, works through all, and is present in all. Everything you are and think and do is permeated with Oneness. (Eph 4:4-6 The Message)

Unity is not a state of being in full agreement. Rather, it is the combining of parts into a whole without sacrificing the individuality of those parts. It is a state of differences without division in spirit.

---

1. Martin Luther King Jr., "Letter from a Birmingham Jail," *Liberation*, June 1963.

Being unified is not necessarily agreeing on everything, but it requires a harmonious striving toward respect for one another's personhood. The biblical mandate and longstanding struggle for "oneness" requires us to see ourselves in those whom we may consider "other."

Our office recently went through the process of attempting to create "oneness." A member of our ministry team who identifies as queer came out to our office staff a few months after joining us. After she left the office that day, I found myself discussing sexuality with an older member of our team. This new information did not fit into her worldview or her understanding of our new team member; in fact, it clashed with her political and religious perspective. In that moment, she felt confused, off balance, and, in all likelihood, a little bit defensive. The situation required me to respond in the moment. I did not have time to enter into reflection in my office, to consult my spiritual and ministerial mentors, or to study up on biblical debates concerning sexuality. The situation required me to respond immediately. I had to engage in the messy and difficult process of helping her acknowledge this previously unencountered "otherness" now present within our ministry team.

Ultimately, I asked the discomforted teammate a series of questions. Did she believe our new teammate was dedicated to our work? Did she believe our new teammate was intelligent and helpful? Did our new teammate know the Lord? Did she love our new teammate and enjoy spending time with her? After receiving positive responses on all of these questions, I asked the question that is most important for our purposes: Did the information revealed twenty minutes earlier by the new staff member change any of this for the older co-worker? As I had suspected, nothing had really changed.

However you feel, whatever your position or perspective, the moral imperative in our intersectional lives boils down to living harmoniously with the other. Even if we do not understand or like something, we have to move forward together. The only way forward is to affirm the other, even and especially when we may not understand or agree with them. The truth is, things change when "others" enter into our circle or when we realize that the other has been there all along, and that we may have been doing the othering. We have to figure out what to do with difference when we encounter it, especially when it is encountered within those we love. Oneness is about more than just hanging a flag, posting a hashtag, sharing an article, or repeating a slogan—it's about relationship. It is about our shared humanity and the spirit of God within each and every one of us. In order to affirm the humanity residing in each of us, we must affirm and process the pain of those we have othered. Only then can we begin to build loving and just relationships.

Hearing and Hollering

There's a particular form of lament we find in the Bible: wailing. The term I've employed in my work and in the Ferguson community is "hollering." The most important question we can ask ourselves in becoming EMTs is this: Who is hollering in our community and why?

We need to understand lament, or hollering. It is the primal cry and expression of pain, of abuse, of separation. It is a refusal to be silent when the world systematically denies our existence and humanity. We cannot be quiet. The brothers and sisters who converged on my small community could no longer be quiet. And even when no one is listening or no one is around, each of us must be able to voice our own pain, to express our own hurting self as we understand it. To express our own experiences of pain is an essential act of humanness. Hollering is human.

In the act of listening to another's hollering, the person who hears becomes more human. It isn't until we encounter that hollering that we begin to see ourselves as a part of the oppressive institutions and structures that cause so much pain and grief. Once we see ourselves in the other, or at least as a part of the structures that oppress the other, we are called to respond with radical resistance and love. We are called to be in true empathic solidarity with those who are hollering.

Processing Pain

During the upheaval in my community, I spoke with the mother of a biracial young adult son who said, "When my son says he intends to resist authority [police], my first impulse is to tell him he is wrong because of my fear for his physical being." She quickly followed with a peppering of questions: "What about his spirit? How do I respect his anger and still encourage him to stay safe? How do I prepare him for racism and injustice without it turning into self-fulfilling expectations?" More importantly, the mother proceeded to become introspective: "What is my own fear about...how can my own fear and anger be translated into positive action? What questions can I ask so he can discover his own understanding, not mine?"

After an unprofessional sigh and exclamation of, "Whoa," I commented that it is not wrong to feel. Under no pretense does anyone deserve to lose his or her life. Nor should he or she have his or her personhood ever discounted. Not feeling something is not human. Some have felt moved to respond. Others are immobilized by the weight of their emotions. Many profess their feelings of pain and angst publicly through protest. There are also those who lament privately.

Each of these methods is a uniquely profound and necessary form of expression. For instance, prayer and protest are the voice of the unheard and unexamined. Martin Luther King Jr. noted, "Riot is the language of the unheard,"[2] a rebuttal to the argument that riot was mere emotive and irrational reaction. The aforementioned quip is perhaps the most often tweeted or rehearsed portion of King's explanation, but he also reminded his 1967 audience at Stanford that critiques of rioting equally require critical consideration about causation. In other words, what are the problems and circumstances that provoke such response? People who are hurting need to be affirmed in their hurt; people who are angry need to be affirmed in their anger. There is no one manner in which pained people are to think or act. It is critical for us to remember that, as we strive to lay aside our own assumptions and simply hear the pain of the other. This way of listening and hearing one another is called empathy. Empathy begins not with speaking but with listening.

It is a core value of human relationship and community.

This conversation highlights our inability at times to move or feel. Daily, we struggle to maintain efforts to coexist, understand, listen, trust, or sustain hope in systems, leaders, and practices. This is true whether in Ferguson, Missouri; our family; or our church. Such is the challenge of exercising "courageous compassion." Courageous compassion is risk-taking . . . it is daring to care. Courageous compassion defies convention. Courageous compassion seeks equity and justice through ministering at the margins—demonstrating divine commitment. Respecting that decisions and actions may not produce the results many expect or want—hope is not lost. Justice is promised, and peace will be given. Peace may exist beyond our understanding, but it is not beyond our grasp. Regardless of the outcomes, we are called—for such a time as this—to be courageously compassionate toward all.

This type of solidarity with those expressing their pain requires that we see and believe in our interconnectedness. Thich Nhat Hanh, a Vietnamese monk who lived through the war that tore apart his

---

2. Martin Luther King Jr., "The Other America," April 14, 1967.

country, said, "To be is to inter-be. You cannot be by just yourself alone. You have to inter-be every other thing."[3] Our actions not only affect ourselves but have consequences that are felt by all. At the core of our existence, we are fundamentally tied and thus accountable to one another. Our choice to either hear or ignore those crying out around us has consequences. Our choice to affirm the pain of those who are fighting for justice has consequences. Our choice to join their fight has consequences. We make these choices when we recognize our interconnectedness. This opting for solidarity has positive consequences in and of itself: it moves us toward justice.

Quantum Entanglement

There is a scientific theory that illustrates this idea: quantum entanglement. "At the simplest level, the idea of entanglement is just the idea that two things that are separated in space can still be the same thing," says NPR science reporter Geoff Brumfiel. "You can have an object that exists in two different spaces and is still the same object."[4]

What has newly been discovered is that these particles within objects still remain connected even though they are physically apart—when one particle becomes excited, so does the other.

Hollering, and our responses to it, has the ability to permanently connect us to and transform one another. Once we have become entangled in one another's grief, we are changed. What moves me, moves you; what hurts me, hurts you, what inspires me, inspires you.

We celebrate lament for that. Lament gives voice to our entanglement, and it also inherently—perhaps surprisingly—exudes hope. We must understand the element of hope in lament, and its critical

---

3. Thich Nhat Hanh, *"Interbeing" The Heart of Understanding: Commentaries on the Prajnaparamita Heart Sutra* (Berkeley, CA: Parallax Press, 2009).

4. Geoff Brumfiel, NPR, January 30, 2015, http://www.npr.org/programs/invisibilia /382451600/entanglement.

importance for multiple generations and entire communities of, people who are "permissible victims,"[5] as Francis Woods puts it. People of color have been designated and oppressed, with no negative repercussions for the oppressors. It is permissible and acceptable to kill black and brown children who have no weapons, and in some cases have done nothing legally wrong other than stand up for themselves and demand the respect of their personhood. It is acceptable to designate particular groups or individuals as intrinsically less valuable, fair game for treatment that would never be considered acceptable for other groups. It is okay even to kill them with no consequence.

Historically, the only folk deemed off-limits are heterosexual, white, wealthy men. This is the only group that seems to be "safe" from the chaos of unaccountability. This is the only group that has been able to consistently rely on trustworthy resolutions, where unjust actions against them generally result in some sort of just consequences. This is our current reality. We are not living as though we are not entangled, or only minimally so and in very few places.

How do we have hope in the midst of this reality?

It makes you wanna holler, and throw up both of your hands.

Hope in the Midst of Hollering

How long have we devalued the lives of black and brown people? How long has our country given us a reason to holler in anger? Too long. W. E. B. Du Bois famously said that "the problem of the twentieth century is the problem of the color line,"[6] and it is fair to say that this problem has extended to the twenty-first century. While that may be disheartening, maddening even, it is possible to find another strand

---

5. Elaine Brown Crawford, *Hope in the Holler: A Womanist Theology* (Louisville: Westminster, 2002), xi.

6. W. E. B. Du Bois, *The Souls of Black Folk* (Chicago: A. C. McClurg & Co., 1903).

of hope in the midst of the hollering when we commit ourselves to what Martin Luther King Jr. called the long arc of justice.

In Ferguson and Baltimore, we saw T-shirts that read "This is not your momma's civil rights movement." That's true, and it's empowering for new and young people who are finding their way and their voices. However, the roots of the injustices are the same, so the movements are inherently connected. That connection must be made in order to understand the scope of the issue and the scope of the pain. We struggle to tell and translate our communities' hollering stories, in part, because we have an entire generation who references history as "then" and "them." We may clearly see the injustice occurring now, in our context, but we don't always connect the here and now to the history of systemic injustices in our country. We too often regard our own history as irrelevant, forgetting our connectedness to those past events. In the church, how do we come to know something and someone that we've never seen? By hearing. How do we hear? There will be a preacher. But here's the problematic truth: most clergy have never been taught the skills or theories to help people tell or retell their stories.

So with that in mind, we need to ask again: Who is hollering, and what does it look like?

How the Church Can Improve Its Hearing

It won't be terribly difficult to find. This type of lament—hollering—is not just vocal; it is physical as well. In their state of distress and grief, the people of Ferguson didn't curl up in a corner; they took to chucking stuff. And as they did so, they were crying. Culturally, traditional white Wesleyan spaces rarely practice lament. Following a presentation at a United Methodist theological school on the East Coast, I was asked by a young white seminarian, "Why don't white people understand hollering?" Most folk see the world through a lens prescribed to their liking, oriented to their own point of view. Thus, many watched the events in Ferguson and what registered with them was that "those" people were throwing things, "rioting," and blocking interstate traffic. The unusual actions registered, but the pain behind the actions, for many viewers, did not.

When we don't understand hollering, it is because we have not had our consciousness sufficiently raised or attuned to the challenges present in our community. Hollering is the expression of people in pain, who have not been heard or respected. As a nation we've ignored for generations the hollered demands for freedom and justice, and today we fail to hear the pain that this has naturally wrought. The church fails to hear the truth that large segments of society are more concerned with their own security and maintaining the status quo than about justice and humanity.

So, who has America failed to hear? To whom is the church shutting its ears?

Hearing the hollering is central to our call to be EMTs because it pulls us out of our comfort zones and into the places where our people need us most. It sometimes calls us out of our churches and into the streets. It's easy to talk about chapel in the chapel. The public space is more intimidating because, whether we like it or not, it's often political. That is where the decisions are made about the appropriation and distribution of money and other resources. That is where decisions are made about who will have power to control spaces and places, and who will have institutional authority over groups of people. That is where decisions are made about what information is shared, and how, and by whom. We tend to see the church as apolitical, but when we as church leaders choose to sit on the sidelines, we are making a political state-ment: your hollering does not concern us.

Of course, you do not always have to go out in the streets to enact justice; you can start in your sanctuary. Your work should be where you are, but reach beyond yourself. Our work as ministry leaders cannot be absent of scripture, but it also can't be absent from the call toward the collective good and the experience of the people who are hollering in our communities. We cannot sit in silence in the church and forget to sit in protest by our sisters and brothers who are in anguish, hollering for justice in the public sphere. We can't look on from afar and tell people who are struggling what to say or do. If we've got something better to say, they'll say it with us if we stand with them. In short, we can't say nothing if we ain't did nothing.

But how do we sing the Lord's song in a strange, nonfamiliar, and nonpromised place? Hope. We need to stand with the lamenters, and sing with them, but we must have hope in the not yet. Hope has been a part of this fight for centuries. In the time of slavery the hope was for the possibility of freedom and realization of the slaves' humanity. In the era of emancipation, the hope was for their voice to be heard. In the contemporary era, it is the hope for equity, for recognition of the oppressed and for their autonomy. In this time of radical responsive-ness identified as the Black Lives Matter era, hope in the possible is found along the same continuum of everything that has come before, but it doesn't just exist in our comfortable spaces. Hope is about the here and now and looking toward the not yet. That's why we can't wait any longer. That is why now is the moment when we decide to do what is right, what we've been called to do. It is our duty to engage, to pull ourselves up, dispense with excuses and rationales, to live into our ought-ness as leaders and help others do the same. Not later. Now. We can't wait for the next election cycle, for the next Flint-like crisis, for the next brother or the next sister to be violated and left for dead.

Ultimately, when we talk about pastoring people, our call—our responsibility—is not only to serve the fifty people (or however many) in our church. There's a constituency and congregation, obviously, but we seem to focus on them exclusively. Christ was given over for the liberation of those who were most disenfranchised, disconnected, and disengaged from the faith community and abused by the systems in which they lived. His ministry was always with a greater orientation toward the masses—even as he was engaged with individuals at any particular time. So, whatever our focus in our parish, we must be raising our congregation's consciousness—their level of alertness to what's happening all around them.

The Picture

During the upheaval in my community, a photograph was taken of me trying to calm a young black man named Joshua. I was not trying to discourage his protest. Instead, I was seeking to affirm that young man in a moment when we were both being disaffirmed by the systems around us. In that moment, I just embraced him. He was so angry, and you could feel it in his body, you could hear it in his speech. Something just said to me, "Grab him. Hold him." Maybe, initially it was to hold him back, but ultimately it was to become symbolic of the situation of that moment and many more that followed. My arms affirmed his existence and our experience.

People who are hurting need to be affirmed in their hurt; people who are angry need to be affirmed in their anger. Let me say it like this: I needed that as much as he needed that. We kept each other from harm's way and from doing something that we would need *not to do*.

I told him, "If you're going to fuss and cuss and be mad, I want you to do it with me. Do it in my ear." And at the same time, I just began to pray with him and to say, "God, give him the strength—give us the strength—to be courageous enough not to do what they expect us to do."

I had not met that young man before that day, but I've met many like Joshua in my lifetime. I was eighteen once, and a young black male. I have a son that we are dutifully nurturing into a man. Joshua's hollering, and that of many more on that day, is entangled in my life, my history, and my hope. People may not understand, but many of us look to the eyes of young people—regardless of color or people's negative assumptions. We see a human being. We see ourselves.

We are all related. We are all responsible for each other. We are bonded together for a common purpose: to live lovingly and justly together. However, we must be truly present with one another first. We must be ready to encounter the other on their own terms. We must be willing to ask ourselves who is hollering around us. How do our own biases and prejudices affect our ability to hear? How do we stay with the hollering until it transforms?

Affirmation as a Manifestation of Grace

When we look in the mirror and see not only ourselves but also the "other," that is a manifestation of grace. Our listening—our attention to stories—is a manifestation of grace. It's in the story of grace and the listening to each other that we begin to acknowledge the justice-related challenges all around us and affirm those who are marginalized, oppressed, and silenced in our churches and communities.

Go into your community and be with the devalued ones. Have conversations. Ask questions about what they feel, what they experience. Admit to them your feelings of fear or inadequacy or whatever. Tell them you want to understand—that you want to help. Tell them how you're feeling it with and for them. *If* we get enough people thinking, feeling, and behaving this way, then the system will begin to change. Because people's hearts will have changed.

Reflection Questions

1. What does respectful conversation look like?

2. Who is hollering around us? What does that hollering look like?

3. How can we seek to hear the voices on the margins and be present with them?

From One Corner
Centers of Trust
James E. Page Jr.

Achieving equity in academic medicine is an uphill battle. The fact that ethnic/racial minorities continue to be underrepresented in senior-level academic ranks, on boards of trustees, and within executive levels in academic medicine has been at times blamed on a lack of genuine effort when it comes to institutional diversity strategies and leveraging resources. Chief diversity officers (CDOs) need to think how to leverage their unique positions. As minorities in the C-Suite, CDOs must choose their battles carefully, as many of the issues they are asked to weigh in on are extremely sensitive and hotly debated.

James E. Page Jr. serves as vice president and chief diversity officer for Johns Hopkins Medicine. Johns Hopkins is one of the world's premier, integrated health systems, with six hospitals, four community-based health-care and surgery centers, and over thirty primary health-care sites throughout Maryland, Washington, DC, and Florida. Setting the tone for academic excellence in medicine and capturing the top-tier ranking among all leading hospitals in the United States for twenty-two years, Hopkins has become respected for its patient care, research, and clinical educational successes. The institution was founded in 1867 as the first American research university, with funds bequeathed by Johns Hopkins, a Quaker merchant who sought to create a university-based health center that would provide care to all people, "regardless of sex, age, color or ability to pay."

As protests erupted on the streets of Baltimore, Page's advice and leadership were called on. Together, leaders of Johns Hopkins agreed that the health and well-being of their institution are inextricably tied to the physical, social, and economic well-being of their city. They agreed not to simply reside in the community but rather embody it: their challenges and successes reflect those of their community. More than one-quarter of Johns Hopkins employees come from eighteen of the most economically depressed zip codes in the state. The hospital's employees and their families face housing, educational, and systemic environment challenges impacting their entire quality of life.

With this realization, Page and his team set to reaffirm their commitment to demonstrating the pivotal role that academic health centers play in improving the social determinants of health in urban neighborhoods. To start with, Johns Hopkins leadership surveyed faculty and staff, asking, "What are the opportunities for Johns Hopkins in engaging with the city we love and serve?" Although responses varied, they heard a resounding call to level the economic playing field. They assembled seven task forces with diverse mandates but with a single goal of strengthening families and neighborhoods by creating better opportunities.

To that end, leadership launched HopkinsLocal, which directs substantial resources into local businesses. Page and other Johns Hopkins team members drew on the expertise of neighborhood residents and community stakeholders to intensify existing programs in education, working to eliminate health disparities and strengthening economic vitality through hiring programs and job training.

Johns Hopkins has also intensified its efforts to improve the future for children, youth, and families of East Baltimore through the Baltimore Scholars Program that offers full scholarships to high-achieving Baltimore City public or charter school students accepted into Johns Hopkins University. The Dunbar Hopkins Health Partnership, a creative collaboration between the high school and multiple divisions of the Johns Hopkins institutions, aims to expand the educational pipeline and ultimately increase the number of talented, underrepresented health professionals and biomedical scientists to ensure workforce diversity in the health-care industry.

Diversity is integral to the excellence and success of any institution, but it is vital for academic health centers. Its promise is essential in delivering extraordinary experience in health care to patients, employees, volunteers, trainees, communities, and suppliers. If managed well, diversity helps bring organizational success. However, change is daunting. Yes, injustices in society are extremely hard to solve. CDOs have an obligation to set goals that will stretch their institutions, communities, cities, and country to embrace their differences. Serving as champions of equity and holding institutions accountable will help strengthen their reputations and trustworthiness.

Just like places of worship, academic health settings can and should be centers of trust. These are places where persons come to be mended, healed, and made whole again. We may not completely understand how or why these places of trust work, but there is a trust...faith that makes the word from a spiritual leader and the works from a physician wonderful. Such places are meant to accept all of God's created when they have nowhere else to turn, providing them with a safe haven where respect, dignity, and trust prevail. When centers of trust fail to meet these expectations, the wounds run extremely deep, impairing the relationship between the institution and the community it professes to serve. Bruised trust can take generations to restore. Hence, the importance of leveraging these centers and upholding their promises of respect, dignity, and trust for all.

Chapter Five
ACT

Before we can move even one step in the direction of ethical pro-phetic witness, we have to allow ourselves to be drawn to some-thing that matters—in our own community. We have to get over our fear of commitment, recognize the reality of our own inaction and our (usually) intentional state of immobilization, and decide to remedy our indifference. This doesn't mean we start manufacturing ministry; rather, we should mine what's already there.

If your church is in an upper-middle-class suburb of white fami-lies, trying to address racism in that community probably will be a different task than it would in a different type of congregation. People in your white congregation have never been on the receiving end of racism. Many—maybe most—members are probably unaware of the ways they participate in racism. They likely do not see the embedded societal structures that ensure the continuity of white privilege, and almost surely do not see their place in those structures. Can you predict how this type of congregation would respond to forceful sermons, class curricula, or new ministries aimed at "curing" them of their racism?[1]

---

1. Adam Hamilton, *Speaking Well: Essential Skills for Speakers, Leaders, and Preachers* (Nashville: Abingdon, 2015), 69.

So, what does it look like for a pastor or other leader to begin addressing racism in the predominately white church? Ponder this: What might happen if you begin to address the congregation's underlying anxieties, those inner points of pain in their lives that provide fertile ground for the nurturing of racism and all kinds of "other-ing"? What if you were to preach, teach, and organize supportive ministries to confront your congregation's issues of fear, resentment, self-deception, self-orientation, and loneliness? What if you began to address head-on the concepts of privilege, cultural and societal power structures, and the emptiness of the American Dream? We need to do ministry on our own corner, with the people and circumstances God presents to us there.

Likewise, ethical prophetic witness doesn't consist of a field trip. You can't simply carry a liberation message out of your own community and congregation, take it to some other community, and expect your message to create change for the people of that community. Prophets are embedded in their own communities. They're indigenous. They have relationships and, therefore, some emotional equity to draw on in difficult conversations. We have to be prophetic in our own circles, not across town or across the globe. We have to work to hear the hollering in our own communities. We have to be awakened to the need and hurt that exist within our own neighborhoods, not just to the injustice that occurs across the globe. The mission of our churches and ministries must address the needs of our own particular communities, not just the needs of those in communities we travel to during designated "mission" trips.

God's justice is focused on uplifting, empowering, and liberating the least, lost, and left behind. An injustice anywhere at any time is an insult and stumbling block to the achievement of justice everywhere, even in the church house! Like Jesus we are called of God to proclaim that justice be present.

How to ACT as a Preacher

Secretly, we preachers see sermons in everything, everywhere, and in everyone; good or bad, rightly or wrongly. Preachers' styles of sermonizing are vast, and our ways and means of crafting compositions vary. But the aim to proclaim glad tidings or good news is the same. We face a struggle of aligning and articulating ancient expressions and mystery into a twenty-first-century, high-definition, multi-sensory, snap-chat, instant fact-check reality. How does one see the dragged-lock, desert-tanned, sandal-wearing Jesus of then, in light of mix-raced Obama in Toms and Tom Ford suits of today? The people sitting in the pews of our churches on Sunday carry in their long-held assumptions about what the world is and who God is. Increasingly, those assumptions seem to be at odds with newly emerging realities. And that makes a lot of folks uncomfortable, unsettled in their lives and in their faith. Handed down by mentors and first conceptualized by Samuel Proctor, "it is the work of aiding those drowning in their is-ness struggling to reach the shores of their ought-ness."[2]

My prescriptive lens as a preacher is framed by dialectical reflection and practice. Dialectic is the art of investigating or discussing the truth of opinions. Such is a principle challenge of preaching. A traditional formulaic of African American homiletics is antithesis, thesis, relevant question and strategic spiritual response. Antithesis is the recognition or acknowledgment of one's existential reality or what is happening in real time. This is what Proctor defines as is-ness. Proctor's counterpoint ought-ness is a reference to what should and is promised to be. This is of exceptional importance to Christian ideals given that God is the source of those promises and that vision what "should be." In dialectical preaching thesis is the good news or expectation and assurance

---

2. Ought-ness for purpose of this project is understood as the embodiment of what we should be and what God has promised we will be (*Circuit Rider*, May/June/July 2016).

guaranteed of God. Thesis is the opposite of what is happening; it is what should, is necessary, and is mandated to be for righteousness' sake. The inherent tension between what is and what should or could be is debatable and ambiguous. This leaves us to wrestle in our preaching with the relevant question or pressing interrogative.

As preachers, we must do some sorting out of these questions about what the "should be" looks like. We must illuminate the picture of God's expectations for us and our communities to the best of our ability. Our sermons should reiterate God's assurances. They should articulate the steps and changes that are necessary in order for us to fulfill God's mandate. We must demonstrate and describe the details of God's righteousness. We must show folks the "should be." Lastly, our strategic spiritual response is to act. Our sermons can point to the called-for actions. They can inspire and compel our hearers to join in the actions. They can deliver specific calls for particular action, literally signing people up for spiritual response.

How to ACT as a Leader

The National Association of Social Workers created a code of ethics to articulate basic values and ethical principles. According to this code of ethics, social work is rooted in six values: service, social justice, the dignity and worth of the person, the importance of human relationships, integrity, and competence. While the work of the pastor and the believer is not the same as the work of a social worker, I posit that these six values put forth by the NASW also correspond to the values at the heart of ministerial work.

Six Values for Action

Service	Ministry	Ministry is meeting the needs of the people in their condition with unconditional love.
Social Justice	Radical Love in Public	Our belief requires us to carry the love of God into the public sphere. It requires us to address the things that are not right nor righteous in our community.
Dignity and Worth of the Person	Sacredness of Person	The Spirit of God is in each person. This entitles them to inalienable rights and the respect of their dignity.
Importance of Human Relationships	"Beloved" Community	We do not believe in a vacuum but rather exist as a communal unit. We depend upon one another for our physical, spiritual, and emotional well-being.
Integrity	Righteousness	Righteousness is not perfection but rather right alignment with the will, way, and witness of God through Jesus Christ.
Competence	Spiritual Giftedness	We each have been divinely gifted, with a specific call and/or task to do.

These values ultimately create a framework for self-reflection that can help us determine how to respond to injustice that we find in our own communities. There isn't a single list or set of steps that we can take to root out injustice. None of us can "fix" everything. It is not

71

our responsibility to overturn systems that have been constructed over generations. Instead, we must determine our own spheres of control influence and the needs in our community in order to find where and how to act.

The Action Framework

When we are ready to become EMTs, when we are ready to live out our love through action, we can use this framework to determine what specific actions we can take:

Ministry: What are the existing ministries within our church? Who are they serving? What needs do our ministry respond to?

Radical Love in Public: Does our ministry touch those outside our doors? Does it address the needs of those we encounter in our immediate public sphere—our neighborhood, our county, local schools, and so forth? What needs exist?

Sacredness of Person: Are there spaces/places in which the sacredness of person is not respected in our community? Where can our church respect the sacredness of those who are other?

"Beloved" Community: What other community members and stakeholders can we partner with? Who can we be in solidarity with?

Righteousness: Are our actions in line with the will and way of God? Where might our own privilege or blindness to the spirit of others be getting in our own way? Are there any additional forces of oppression that we need to interrogate or address?

Spiritual Giftedness: What gifts, resources, and talents does our church have? What do we have to offer others?

Using the Framework: An Example

In 2016 I met with a congregation in Seattle to discuss how to act in the face of injustice. Over the course of the day, we ended up discussing a nearby marijuana dispensary that opened next door to an after-school program designed to keep kids off of drugs and out of gangs. The white congregation was understandably concerned. The shop may have been legal, but it surely would not have been allowed to open so close to a location that served a white population.

Many members of the congregation were ready to spring into action. They quickly started brainstorming action steps they could take. "I could speak at a town hall meeting!" "I know someone in local government we can talk to!" "Maybe we should start a petition!" These suggestions were well intentioned, but were not attentive to the needs, feelings, or experiences of those who were most affected by the opening of this store. We began to walk through this process together. Following is a summary of the process and key conclusions.

Ministry: We discussed the church's current and past ministry efforts around racial and economic divides. We recognized that these ministries did not attract a racially diverse audience and began to ask why this was the case.

Radical Love in Public: We asked who was missing from the conversation and found that we needed to become more aware of the feelings, needs, and experiences of those who were most affected by the store's opening. We discussed the importance of becoming more attentive to the needs of the racial and economic other.

Sacredness of Person: We determined that the opening of the store without community approval violated the sacredness of the families and children who participated in the after-school program.

"Beloved" Community: We brainstormed a list of community partners that we needed to learn from and work with in order to address this communal injustice. We included the founder and staff of the after-school program, local churches that serve the racial and economic other, families that live in the neighborhood, and those who participated in the program.

Righteousness: We interrogated our own positions of privilege to try to determine where our lingering blind spots were located.

Spiritual Giftedness: We left the congregation to determine how their particular gifts could be used to stand in solidarity with those who were experiencing oppression and marginalization in this instance.

This process is difficult and messy. We may often feel tempted to give up or slide back to simple, one-size-fits-all, packaged forms of addressing injustice. However, the truth is, we can only create real change when we are willing to do the hard work of listening, recognizing our own biases. It can only happen when we are willing to do work with others and when we commit the time necessary. Creation of a just ministry does not happen overnight. It is not something we do for one Sunday or one season. *Act*ing requires us to create a permanent and consistent change not only within our institutions but also within ourselves.

Dare to Care

Simply put, acting—caring—is the practice of being with and standing for those unable to do so themselves. If you see a brother, or a community, lying hurt on the street, you've got to walk right up to that place of hurt and pick up a corner of the mat. You've got to decide to care. I dare you to care.

Reflection Questions

1. What can we do as individuals to be an Empathic Model of Transformation in our own context?

2. What might we need to do to educate ourselves about larger systems so that we can empathically and ethically relate to "the other"?

3. How can you use your privilege, whatever that looks like, to act as a blessing for others?

From One Corner
Creating Gravity for Christ
Rich Daniels

My colleague Rich Daniels is a social entrepreneur who often shares with me the idea of "creating gravity." This concept is centered around bringing intellectual and social capital into space and connection with each other and in doing so, employing the best of all these resources to create footing that makes possible greater work that encourages innovation and support in risk-taking or death-defying acts.

As a leader in the sports marketing world, Rich developed a high-end unique product in sports apparel that targeted both the elite athletes and the weekend warrior. While creating an innovative and useful product in a competitive space, what became apparent was the emphasis on brand and the relationships that good and reputable branding builds and requires. You have to have relationships with those who are doing innovative work around you in order to be successful.

He's taken those successful business practices and asked what it would look like to apply and appropriate those practices in the social and spiritual world. What would it look like to bring different innovative, insightful, and inspiring people together and create something new in the social and spiritual world?

When thinking about community, especially in the context of Christian community, we know what we have in common—Christ. We are disciples or followers of Christ.

As a community we are drawn together or pulled together by a common belief and love of Jesus Christ. But how do we love God and love one another? How do we "make disciples of Jesus Christ for the transformation of the world"?

You may have heard the song "They'll Know We Are Christians by Our Love."

How are others drawn to Christ by our acts of love, acts of faith? Authentic relationships are built by closing the distance between ourselves and others. It can happen by our stepping closer to someone or by them stepping closer to us. Why would someone step closer to us? Have you ever met someone to whom you were "drawn"? What was it about them? Did they tell great stories? Did they listen well?

The four people who carried the mat of the sick man to Jesus brought their efforts together and, by doing so, aligned themselves in concern for the hurt one and in the committed effort to get the hurt to a source of help and hope. The key element is creating gravity. Gravity relies on the scientific truth that matter attracts other matter. In the same way, big ideas attract other big ideas. When these big ideas come together, they can lead people to hope and healing.

"Creating gravity for Christ" means drawing people close to him through actions and words. What could you do, within your sphere of influence, to bring different people together? To bring different groups together? What can you do to create gravity for Christ?

CONCLUSION

We must learn how to pray with our feet. I'm a runner, and in the face of the events of August 2014, I began a practice of running from my home in Ferguson to the Canfield Apartments where a young man was killed and laid in the street, unattended and uncared for, for four hours. I go to be reminded of what happened. I go because in my tradition, the place of death is where life began. Where there is hurt, healing took place. I go to that place to remind me of the work I have to do. The prize isn't to be in first, second, or third place. The prize is to finish the race.

Runners' workouts often consist of roadwork. Runners, unlike cyclists, are trained to run opposite or against traffic patterns. They do this so that they are acknowledged by oncoming traffic. It is interesting to watch how cars either fail to notice or at the last minute work to evade runners, like myself. For me, honoring this practice is not only a technique for self-preservation, but it serves as a personal act of resistance. Wearing bright-colored tennis shoes and remaining non-deferential to cars, buses, and trucks says, "These are my streets too." Every stride is a refrain of the civil rights hymn "We Should Not Be Moved." The action of running in the street is a personal protest. This protest is a signaling of the injustice that exists in a community where you can be legally and justifiably stopped and subsequently killed for not walking on sidewalks—sidewalks that remain in disrepair or that don't actually exist.[1]

Existentialism, or the questions of human experience, presents those of us in ministry with two pressing realities. First is the necessity of ministry to meet the needs of people in their condition with unconditional love and a tremendous expectation to create change through empathic presence. Second is the prophetic dimension of ministry, which concentrates on speaking and living out the truth of God to God's people. A prophet endeavors to declare divine truth by means of unmasking the reality of the world's condition and pointing to the promise of God's infinite love, care, compassion, and justice. Such witness is committed to addressing social injustice by respecting the sacredness of each person and community. Its objective is to instill, sustain, and restore hope! Hope is the indication of certainty in the fulfillment of what ought to be, and a desire for much more, but with no real assurance of getting it. Hope as described in scripture is best understood as confident expectation in those things we have not seen nor received.

Thus, our challenge is not to ignore. The practice of avoidance, or an unwillingness to recognize what is wrong, inequitable, or unjust is unacceptable. Failing to *acknowledge* is unconscionable, and intentional disregard is criminal. At the same time, we are charged with daring to inspire. That is, we are charged to fill someone with the urge or the ability to do or feel something, especially to do something creatively. Hence Booker T. Washington instructed, "If you want to lift yourself up, lift someone else up!"[2]

---

1. This is a reference to an explanation for the initial encounter between Officer Darren Williams and Michael Brown Jr. in August 2014.

2. Booker T. Washington. BrainyQuote.com, Xplore Inc, 2016. http://www.brainyquote .com/quotes/quotes/b/bookertwa382202.html, accessed September 23, 2016.

The struggle is that we're looking for some sort of formula to help us know what to do and when we should do it and how to go about it. *But there is no particular way.* The men who helped the paralytic were likely on their way to someplace else. Still, they stopped, picked up the hurt one, and took him to Jesus.

In regard to race, our congregations must recognize that the divides and disconnects that come about because of privilege are problematic because they reflect our lack of love. As disciples we are supposed to—ought to—love one another. It's how people will know we are followers of Christ—by our love. It's what Christ told and showed us how to do.

If we want to not only talk the talk but also walk the walk, this should be of great concern for the church. Historically, however, it simply has not been of great concern. People do not want to acknowledge the reality that we have a historical imprint of violence and hatred. The demeaning and devaluing of persons spans out generation to generation to generation before us. That indelible imprint on society—historically, systemically, and culturally—has now been memorialized and systematized through our institutions, and has become our DNA.

Our attitudes and our behaviors are natural—nearly instinctive—and they have a direct impact on culture. The concerns in our communities are issues of humanity. In other words, because they disproportionally affect some people, they affect all of us. As long as we remain naïve that fact and refuse to look within ourselves as Christ's body and to hold one another accountable, we will not be effective models of transformation.

Great responsibilities cry out to us. They scream out to us. They are yelling so loudly. Hesitation and procrastination are no longer an option. You and I can no longer sit down on padded pews of complacency and apathy, looking down our hypocritical noses. This world's cry of lament hearkens us to remember the adage "But by the grace of God, there go you and I."

The aim and modes of ethical prophecy in the twenty-first century should be pressing us toward the development of new knowing, language, and leadership. We have to acknowledge that there is something really wrong. We have to affirm the personhood and significance of each and every one of us. And we have to decide and dare to act lovingly and justly.

Blessed is the burden to answer the call. The call requires personal sacrifice. The call demands toil. The call demands love. The call demands we do justice. It is a responsibility to engage and confront every injustice and act of violation exercised against any part of humanity and creation. This is the prophetic task of truth and justice. The prophetic task is responsible for bringing faith into the public square.

If we are going to respond to our call toward prophetic witness, we must strive to lift up every voice. We must work to uplift every block, barrio, and hood. We must reexamine misguided, oppressive, and abusive theological and social constructs. We must be committed to development of healthy, loving, and just relationships and practices; these must be directed toward liberation for each and all. And we must take a deep breath, and recognize that each one of us can answer the call where we are, as we are. You or I cannot achieve it all, or all at once. This journey for me began in 2014, when I was able and ready to do *one thing, on one day*. You are able and ready too.

It is going to get better. God's promises will be fulfilled. I run and run and run in that street, facing traffic, and I hope that others will run with me. I hope you will run with me, and that together we will get to the promised place.

Keep on celebrating the one who deserves all the praise. There is one who deserves expressions of reverence, one who deserves our acts of worship. Let us keep on ascribing all glory, majesty, power, and domain to the right one. Forever and ever! As we progress, let us remember to keep on, keeping on.

Part Three

PRACTICAL HELPS

SUGGESTED NEXT STEPS

Suggested Next Step #1: Holding Up Your Corner: Guided Conversations about Race

Holding Up Your Corner: Guided Conversations about Race is a resource to help pastors and other faith leaders address issues of race and inequity in their communities. It is a six-hour group experience, with a facilitator's guide, participant books, and DVD including video content for each conversation segment. It includes the presentation of key content via brief video clips, activities and guided discussion in small groups around tables, and times for sharing with the whole group. It is available at cokesbury.com, amazon.com, or your favorite bookseller.

The facilitator's guide is available for download at www.Abingdon Press.com/HoldingUpYourCorner. To lead the Guided Conversation, you will need a participant book for every person in your group, the facilitator's guide, and the DVD.

What follows is an excerpt from the facilitator's guide, to help you begin planning the Conversation for your community:

Leading the Guided Conversation about Race

Leading conversations about difficult topics such as race can be a little scary, but anyone who approaches this work with a loving heart and an open mind can facilitate a conversation. You don't need to be an expert; you don't even need to have facilitated this sort of conversation before. The tips below can help individuals at all knowledge levels to facilitate the *Holding Up Your Corner* conversation or a similar conversation of your own design.

Getting Started

- There may be someone in your church or group who is better suited to the task of leading this conversation than you are. If that is the case, ask and empower that person, and assist in all the ways that you are able.

- Other faith leaders in your community may have done this before. If you need support or help, ask someone with experience to come alongside you the first time you lead this conversation. Or ask them for advice and encouragement as you prepare.

- BUT, do not spin your wheels in thinking and preparing and discussing in advance. Know that you will probably make some mistakes, or say something not quite the way you intend. That is OK! Give yourself permission to do what you can, and know that God will use it. The main thing is simply to take the authority that you have been given, to act.

Preparing

- Get the dates on your calendar! For many of us, just deciding to do something and making the commitment is half the battle. Don't wait until you are "ready." You will never feel ready, but if you believe this conversation is important, you will find that you have what you need.

- Before facilitating this conversation, examine your own biases on the topic to ensure that you can remain neutral while leading discussion. Remind yourself to remain neutral throughout the experience. Model active listening.

- Study materials thoroughly before facilitating a dialogue. Pastors and other faith leaders should read *Holding Up Your Corner: Talking About Race in Your Community*, by F. Willis Johnson and *Fear of the Other: No Fear in Love*, by Will Willimon. These books will provide foundational understanding, empowering you to lead wisely.

- Be ready for the event physically, spiritually, mentally, and emotionally, so that you will have stamina and grace. Your preparation will set the tone.

Inviting

- Extend an open invitation to your congregation and the broader community. Include people from education, health care, city government, civic organizations, law enforcement, business, and so on. Make the invitation for all, not just hand-selected people in your community. Or—if that seems too much to take on, hold the first Conversation (or two or three) with leaders in your congregation, or perhaps your leaders and those from another church in your area. Those leaders can then share about their experiences with others in the church and community, laying the groundwork for you to lead subsequent conversations with a broader group.

- Offer some way for people to register, so that you can prepare accordingly. You may choose to set up a Facebook event, and ask people to "join" it.

Logistics and Hospitality

- Host the conversation in a room that is large enough to hold the number of people you expect to attend.

- The room should have a sound system with microphone for the facilitator, a way to play the video clips (DVD), and a way to display presentation slides, if you are using them (included in the *Holding Up Your Corner* resources).

- Consider reserving a room at a local school, a hotel banquet room, or other venue, especially if your church facility won't accommodate the event.

- Participants should be seated at round tables for six or—at the most—eight people. You may also use long tables, and have people sit across from one another in groups of four.

- We do not encourage assigned or manipulated seating for the conversation. It is best to allow people to self-seat. However, as people arrive for the event you might encourage them to sit with people they do not know, rather than their friends or the people they came with. Make the suggestion, but let people sit where they are comfortable, and don't make it a big deal.

- The event will last around six hours. It's best to do this all in one day, but it can be done in two separate sessions over two days.

- Be sure to start and end at the publicized times. But plan a forty-five-minute window before and after the event, for gathering and refreshments and for visiting.

- The day before the event, set the tables with pens, colored markers, index cards or sticky notes, *Holding Up Your Corner* participant books (one at each seat), and brightly colored sheets of construction paper (one for each person). If budget allows, you might add bright tablecloths and potted plants, snacks or other items.

- Make the room as comfortable as you can; adjust the temperature, lighting, and so on.

- Think through the event and anticipate what your participants might need, and what will make them feel at ease and well cared-for.

- If possible, have two extra microphones to pass around the room for group sharing times.

- Enlist volunteers to serve as greeters, to sign people in at a registration/welcome table, to serve refreshments and lunch, to run the audio and video systems, and to clean up after the event. Also have two volunteers ready to pass the microphone around during group sharing.

- The audio technician should play music softly during table discussion times, if possible.

- If budget allows, serve coffee, breakfast snacks, fruit, or other refreshments beginning forty-five minutes before your start time, and have them available throughout the day. Serve lunch, and let participants eat at the tables.

Facilitating the Event

- Before you begin, point out the nearest restrooms and any other helpful notes about the facility and the day's schedule.

- Let participants know that their conversations are not being recorded in any way. Ask them not to use any recording devices. Remind them to silence their cell phones.

- Pause once during the morning session and once during the afternoon session for a brief stretch and bathroom break. Decide in advance where in the conversation you think this will work best, and include this in your facilitator's guide notes.

Guiding the Conversation

- Keep the conversation focused and on schedule. It is important to address questions and allow participants ample time to process their thoughts; however, as facilitator, you must ensure that the conversation stays on topic and that the timeline of the event is adhered to. Think of yourself as the bumper guards in a children's lane at a bowling alley. Give the conversation some leeway, but do not let it get out of the lane.

- Ensure all participants feel comfortable enough to contribute. Invite quiet participants to speak up, and/or encourage participants who dominate the circle to listen to others.

- Handle any issues, tensions, or conflicts that arise by moving the conversation. If something troubling is said, give other participants the chance to address it (example: Does anyone have a different opinion?). It may be helpful for you to rephrase comments to achieve clarity (example: I believe you are saying _____. Is that what you meant?).

- Consider providing a Conversation Covenant to keep the conversation productive and grounded in your common faith. (A sample covenant is included in the *Holding Up Your Corner: Guided Conversations* facilitator's guide.) Review the covenant at the beginning of each session and refer to it when necessary. For example: "Let's look again at our covenant, which asks us to give everyone a chance to speak before sharing a second time."

- Ensure that the conversation is oriented around dialogue rather than debate. Debate focuses on **winning** while dialogue focuses on **finding and exploring common ground and understanding**. Encourage participants to keep an open mind, to listen to opinions that differ from their own, and to **seek to understand rather than influence** one another.

Continuing the Conversation

- At the end of the session, ask participants to complete a brief evaluation form, so that you can improve the conversation for next time. Also plan a time to debrief the session with a few colleagues or participants.

- Facilitate a way for next steps and continued connection to happen. This should be contextual, in ways that make sense and are comfortable for your community. You might agree together to set a date for a second conversation, including new people. You might set up smaller ongoing action groups, based on conclusions made by participants at the event. You may ask someone to set up a closed group on Facebook or another social media site, where people can continue the conversation and begin to gather around particular actions.

- Consider creating an EMT map of your community. Directions are included in this book and in the *Guided Conversations Participant Book*.

Remember

- Give yourself—and the participants—permission to do and say the "wrong" things. Be comfortable being uncomfortable, and share that expectation with participants. Be courageously vulnerable! Model it for your community, and invite them to lay down their own assumptions and defenses, too. Know that the conversation will be awkward, and be OK with that.

Suggested Next Step #2: Create an EMT Map of Your Community

This next step is a natural progression from the *Guided Conversation About Race*. When that experience ends, most people will be ready and eager to *do something*. Which is precisely the point. This community mapping process is something you can recommend for people to consider. You might decide to organize and lead it yourself. You might tap a staff member or volunteer to lead it. Or you might let the Conversation group determine how to proceed.

What follows is excerpted from the *Guided Conversation Participant Book*. Participants will have what they need to move forward on this next step, with your encouragement and support:

At the end of this Conversation, you are strongly encouraged to find practical ways to Act. As you have learned, the first step is to acknowledge that something is not right. The second step is to affirm the reality of that "not right" experience for others. Following these steps will naturally lead you to actions. We suggest that you do this work by creating a "map" of your community. This is not just a geographical map. It is a process of inquiry and reflection to help your group Acknowledge, Affirm, and then Act. This process will empower you to become Empathic Models of Transformation in your community.

You will first need to determine:

- how to conduct the process,
- how to capture your discoveries and decisions,

- who will commit to the process,
- who will be responsible for what, and
- how/when you will gather to do this work.

Creating an EMT Map

To begin, you will **investigate what is happening** *in your community.* Look for harbingers of change, evidence of need, and signs that some people in your community are being "othered." These may be subtle, even seemingly invisible, things. They may have little to do with race, in fact.

Use your senses, and **follow the clues** they provide. Here's an example: Stand outside and listen—really listen. Do you hear anything new? Is there a louder screech of traffic along the newly widened roadway nearby? Or do you hear a frequent, house-shaking roar of jet engines overhead after a recent change in flight path regulations? What might this mean for the people in your community? How might these sounds be predictors of change, and what are those changes likely to be?

Explore. Inquire. **Pay attention to sensory prompts, and pursue them.** Reflect on what you hear and see, and discuss your reflections as a group. What conclusions can you draw? Do they point you toward particular actions? Decide together how to keep pursuing what to do next.

Continually **pull your focus back to** *people.* As you investigate, ask how real people are affected. Catch yourself when you slip into the habit of considering people as broad groups, and remind yourself that we are all individuals. **Drop your assumptions** about people's backgrounds, self-identity, and experiences. Don't paint all the people who live in one neighborhood with one brushstroke, for instance. This process is about the particularities of real people's lives, not about broadly generalized groups as we see on TV news.

Facts and figures are helpful and can be an important part of your investigation. However, **don't get bogged down or distracted by statistics or demographic information.** Those figures are frozen in a certain time and a certain place. Instead of relying on national statistics, we encourage you to find numbers for your local community. Your

93

local governmental agencies should be able to help, and you should be able to find a lot of data online.

In addition to your sensory investigation, **use the questions below** to create a nuanced and insightful "map" of your community. You will probably need to start with just one or two of these questions. Remember, you cannot fix all the systems and all the wrongs at once. Do what you can. Pursue the questions that seem most important or resonant in your community.

EMT Map Questions

Experiences: How do people experience life in your community?

- Does your local law enforcement reflect the racial make up of your community?

- Does your local law enforcement engage in diversity or de-escalation training?

- Does the leadership of your community reflect the racial makeup of your community?

- How many job opportunities for unskilled workers exist in your community?

- What is the rate of homelessness in your community?

- Is a car required to live in your community?

- What is the average household income in your community? How does this average change when we look at household income by race/gender/sexuality?

- What percentage of your community has been incarcerated?

Environment:

- Does everyone in your community have access to clean water?

- Is the air in your community safe to breathe?

- Does everyone in your community have access to healthy food options? Is a car required to reach these healthy food options? How many families live with food insecurity?

- What percentage of your community owns or rents their living space?

- Have police officers in your area ever been convicted of a crime while on duty? What is the discipline policy of your local law enforcement agency?

- Do all community members feel welcome in all areas of town?

- Are the majority of buildings/public spaces in your community accessible to individuals with disabilities?

Education: How do people gain knowledge and skills in your area?

- Are all of the schools in your community accredited?

- Do the schools in your areas have adequate resources for students with special needs?

- Do the schools in your community offer English as a second language or other English-learning resources?

- What percentage of elementary school students meet grade-level benchmarks in your community?

- What is the graduation and/or drop-out rate of the high-schools in your community?

- Is low-cost or free childcare available in your community?

- Are there free or low-cost preschools in your community?

- Are there free or low-cost job training opportunities in your area?

A GUIDE TO LANGUAGE
AND TERMINOLOGY
ABOUT RACE

We all struggle at times to understand others and to be understood. This section offers some help for thinking about language in matters of race and inequity. First, let's define what we mean by "language." For this discussion, we assume that all the readers and participants are using the same body of words—in this case, English. But language goes beyond that body of words known as English. It is also the signs, symbols, gestures, sounds, shorthand, slang, and lingo used within the general category of English.

Language is tricky, even in families and other close relationships, where people are familiar with and "speak" the same language. It is especially challenging when we don't fully understand the words other people use to describe their experiences.

Another layer of difficulty arises when we are talking about complex systems like economics; education; law enforcement, the justice system, and incarceration; health care; social services; and the church.

The list below offers definitions and explanations of words and phrases that often come up in conversations about race and inequity. You're encouraged to familiarize yourself with these terms so that you can better understand what others are saying and can better express your own thoughts and experiences.

Ally: a person who stands in support of the "other"; typically a member of a dominant group standing beside members of a marginalized group; e.g., a man who advocates for equal pay for women

Bias: a preference for or against, especially one that interferes with impartial judgment. Bias can be conscious or unconscious, meaning we may or may not be aware of our biases.

Bigotry: intolerance of and/or hatred of communities, cultures, religions, races, ethnicities, or political beliefs that differ from one's own

Discrimination: unfair treatment toward an individual or group based on race, sex, color, religion, national origin, age, gender identity, ability, or sexual orientation

Equity vs. Equality: What do these words mean? What is the difference? Why does the author prefer the terms *equity/inequity*?

Equality means that everyone has the same access to resources or the same resources, and *inequality* means that, for some people or groups of people, access to resources is limited or barred. For example, principles of equality deem that every child has access to an education and, further, to the same level of education. Therefore, all schools in all districts would have good teachers and sufficient resources.

Equity is the concept that allocation of resources should be based on the specific needs of different people and groups. With the acknowledgment of the reality of inequality in our societal institutions and structures comes the acknowledgment that some people need more in order to get to the same place as those who started with more. For example, in education, students with disabilities will need more resources and teachers with more specialty education in order to progress at the same rate as typically developing students. Giving students with disabilities access to the same schools and teachers (equality) will not alone "level the playing field."

The author prefers the terms *equity/inequity* over *equality/inequality* because equity requires that we pay attention to the specific needs of individuals and communities and allocate resources accordingly. Acting equitably does not assume that everyone is starting from the same position or place and requires that we care more wholly for "the least of these."

Identity Group: a particular group, culture, or community with which an individual identifies or shares a sense of belonging; e.g., racial identity groups share a racial identity—white people share a white racial identity, while black people share a black racial identity. Identity groups can be formed using any identity (race, class, gender, religious identity, etc.).

Justice: the respect of the protection, provision, and promise that is divinely given to every human being. Justice is the recognition of the *imago dei*, or image of God, that resides in each person. Justice requires us to affirm the dignity that society denies, ensuring that we are accountable for the protection, provision, and promise of our neighbor. Justice requires us to pursue that which is not only right but also righteous. For more on justice, read *A Christian Justice for the Common Good* by Tex Sample.

Language: the words we use. The words we use matter. We must be intentional about the words we use, and we must be willing to change our language as we continue to learn new things and move ourselves toward justice. It is important to define the terms we use and to push others to define the terms that they use in order to pursue right relationship. We acknowledge that language is limited and can be a stumbling block to righteous relationship if we are too firmly affixed to definitions that we assume are shared or universally understood.

Legal Justice: Legal justice requires that each individual receives equal protection under the law. We must work to fix the racial inequities in our legal system, but the pursuit of justice requires us to go further to transform all of the systems that shape our society.

Oppression: severe exercise of power and subjugation that works systematically, institutionally, and interpersonally to privilege one identity group and disadvantage another

Other: The "other" is an individual or community who we think of as somehow intrinsically different from ourselves. The "other" is that which is not us. We are "othering" individuals or communities when we treat them in a manner that differs from how we would treat or interact with those in our own identity groups. For more on "othering," read *Fear of the Other: No Fear in Love* by Will Willimon.

Power: social capital; the ability to determine one's own path or shape the path and experience of others. Like privilege, power is nether good or bad on its own; rather, it is a condition or tool that can be used in positive or negative ways.

Prejudice: pre-judgement; forming an opinion without knowing the facts; a feeling, unfavorable or favorable, toward a person or thing prior to, or not based on, actual experience. A prejudice, unlike a misconception, is actively resistant to all new evidence.

Privilege: advantage or benefits that individuals or groups of individuals enjoy because of their membership in a dominant identity group. Privilege is largely invisible to those who have it. Privilege is neutral: it can be wielded in a way that is either positive or negative. Ex: white privilege, male privilege, class privilege.

Race: historically and socially constructed category used to differentiate people based on physical characteristics such as skin color, eye shape, and hair texture. Race is a man-made category that reflects differences that are only skin-deep.

Racism: unequal treatment of or violence against people or communities because of their race. The abuse of power and privilege by systems or individuals to marginalize individuals who do not fit into the category of whiteness.

Reconciliation vs. Right Relationships: We want to focus on building right relationships rather than reconciliation because we are not repairing something broken; rather, we are creating something new. The term *reconciliation* refers to rebuilding or mending a relationship that was broken, but often relationships across lines of difference didn't exist in the first place. Relationships between white people and people of color cannot be reconciled if they never existed. So when we talk about this work, we talk about building anew. We are building right relationships from the ground up, from the acknowledgment that God is in all persons. We can acknowledge that we are all broken persons and that the reconciliation work needs to be done within. We need to reconcile with who we are and with a God that tells us who we ought to be. In that process of reconciliation, we can begin to build right relationships with those we have "othered."

Responsibility: We can only innately know the reality in which we live. We have to make extra effort to see and experience and understand another's reality. Therefore, oppressors do not innately know the experience of the oppressed, and so, if they are to work with the oppressed to build right relationships, they have to make extra effort to understand a different reality. The danger in this step of building knowledge and relationship is that oppressors too often put the responsibility on the oppressed to teach them about oppression rather than doing the work themselves. They might say, "Come here and tell me about your life and your struggles," instead of "I will come to you and listen and see and be with you." It is the oppressor's responsibility to learn how to no longer be an oppressor. Use the resources around you, not the people who are "under" you.

Social Location: where you sit relative to systems of power. Your social location includes your race, class, gender, sexual orientation, neighborhood, etc. Your social location helps form your unconscious biases as well as personal prejudices.

Social Construct: a label or identity that has been created by humans that are based on perceived categories of difference. When we say race is a social construct, we are referring to the reality that race is a category that was developed throughout our history by cultural, economic, and social systems based on perceived differences. Racial categories are based only on appearance, and not on any genetic or intrinsic difference.

Sphere of Influence: your corner! Your sphere of influence is the space in which you live your daily life and the spaces in which you have the ability to create change. Your sphere of influence includes your family and friends, neighborhood, work environment, church, school, and anywhere else where you invest your time and talents.

Stereotype: an oversimplified conception of a group of people in which all individuals in the group are labeled and often treated based on perceived group characteristics. Ex: referring to or conceiving of young black men as "thugs."

System: a set of forces that shapes our shared reality and enforces, memorializes, and monetizes power. Our reality is shaped by economic, political, and cultural systems that reinforce current balances of power.

Systemic/Institutional Oppression: a nexus in which established laws, customs, and practices systematically reflect and produce inequities based on one's membership in targeted social identity groups.

PRIVILEGE QUIZ

(from *Holding Up Your Corner:*
Guided Conversations about Race)

The Privilege Quiz is an exercise from the *Guided Conversations About Race*. It was developed at the Center for Social Empowerment in Ferguson, Missouri, and is helpful on its own as part of individual and group reflection on race, inequity, and privilege.

The quiz is meant to be a tool to help people reflect on their own life experiences as they compare to the experiences of others. Privilege is often invisible to those that yield it, so this quiz will help you see the areas where you have experienced privilege. This quiz asks a series of yes or no questions regarding your childhood and life experiences. Each answer is labeled (+1) or (-1). These numbers show where structural and societal power lie. Add up your totals to determine how many of your experiences align with positions of power.

This quiz is not to be used to compete in terms of privilege or oppression. It is only meant to help us reflect on how power has shaped our experience to prepare us to authentically and thoughtfully engage with those who may have a different experience.

Did your parents own their home?	Yes (+1)	No (-1)
Did either of your parents graduate from college?	Yes (+1)	No (-1)
Did you grow up watching television characters that generally looked like you?	Yes (+1)	No (-1)
Does anyone in your family struggle with drug or alcohol abuse?	Yes (-1)	No (+1)
Did your family have more than fifty books in the house when you were growing up?	Yes (+1)	No (-1)
Have you ever felt an opportunity or experience was closed to you because you didn't know how to speak, dress, or act?	Yes (-1)	No (+1)
Have you experienced discrimination because of your race?	Yes (-1)	No (+1)
Did your family teach you that police were to be feared?	Yes (-1)	No (+1)
Was your family ever forced to move because your parents could not afford to pay their bills?	Yes (-1)	No (+1)
Have you ever been denied a job or paid less for comparable work, OR not been taken seriously at work, OR had a less qualified man promoted over you because of your gender?	Yes (-1)	No (+1)

Privilege Quiz

Are you able to go to new places without worrying about accessibility?	Yes (+1)	No (-1)
Have you ever been scared to walk down the street holding your partner's hand?	Yes (-1)	No (+1)
Have you ever felt judged or uncomfortable because of the size, height, or shape of your body?	Yes (-1)	No (+1)
Did you take vacation outside your home state before you were eighteen years old?	Yes (+1)	No (-1)
Have you ever inherited, or do you expect to inherit, money or property?	Yes (+1)	No (-1)
Do the people with power in your community look like you?	Yes (+1)	No (-1)
Has anyone asked you to speak for or represent your race?	Yes (-1)	No (+1)
Have you ever lived somewhere that didn't feel safe?	Yes (-1)	No (+1)

Total: _____

HOW TO GET (AND STAY) CONNECTED

www.holdingupyourcorner.com
www.thecenterforsocialempowerment.com

The Center for Social Empowerment, located in Ferguson, Missouri, is a hub for theologically informed reflection, investigation, and education on social and racial justice issues. By providing a variety of diverse learning opportunities, the Center aims to equip Ferguson and other communities with the experiences and tools they need to promote social and racial justice in their own context.

The shooting of an unarmed African American teenager by a police officer on August 9, 2014, sparked sustained protests and media attention in the city of Ferguson, Missouri. In response, Wellspring Church and its pastor, Rev. Dr. F. Willis Johnson Jr., sought to be a safe place for local justice activists as well as to provide necessary dialogue that would echo on radio waves and feature in newspapers across the country.

However, a larger effort was needed to establish positive and sustainable change for the local and national community in the face of this tragedy. One year later on August 9, 2015, the Center for Social Empowerment was officially launched. Its presence provides a neighborhood-based facility for urban education, social enterprise, and engagement that focuses on equity, inclusion, and the transformation of public, private, and community systems. Training is also provided to understand how our faith can be applied to the response and management of injustices such as police brutality and other inequities plaguing different communities. The Center's work focuses on education, enterprise, and engagement.

RECOMMENDED RESOURCES FOR READING, WATCHING, AND LISTENING

Books

America's Original Sin: Racism, White Privilege, and the Bridge to a New America

Jim Wallis offers a prophetic and deeply personal call to action in overcoming the racism so ingrained in American society. He speaks candidly to Christians—particularly white Christians—urging them to cross a new bridge toward racial justice and healing.

A Christian Justice for the Common Good

Tex Sample describes a Christian justice for the common good and what it looks like on the ground in real-world settings. Calling Christians (individuals, as well as communities of faith) to a concrete version of social well-being befitting faithful life in Jesus and God's vision of justice for the world, Tex Sample drills deeper and identifies the skills that must be cultivated to do justice work with others—work that will create a lasting impact while extending a Christian vision for the common good.

Between the World and Me

This series of essays by Ta-Nehisi Coates confronts the notion of race in America and how it has shaped American history, many times at the cost of black bodies and lives. Thoughtfully exploring personal and historical events, from his time at Howard University to the Civil War, the author poignantly asks and attempts to answer difficult questions that plague modern society.

Divided by Faith: Evangelical Religion and the Problem of Race in America
Michael O. Emerson and Christian Smith, who conducted two thousand telephone surveys and two hundred face-to-face interviews in preparing this book, argue that evangelicals have a theological worldview that makes it difficult for them to perceive systematic injustices in society.

Witnessing Whiteness: The Need to Talk about Race and How to Do It
Shelly Tochluck invites readers to consider what it means to be white, describes and critiques strategies used to avoid race issues, and identifies the detrimental effect of avoiding race on cross-race collaborations. Questioning the implications our history has for personal lives and social institutions, the book considers political, economic, socio-cultural, and legal histories that shaped the meanings associated with whiteness.

Waking Up White
For twenty-five years, Debby Irving sensed inexplicable racial tensions in her personal and professional relationships. Then, in 2009, one "aha!" moment launched an adventure of discovery that drastically shifted her worldview and upended her life plan. In *Waking Up White*, Irving tells her often cringe-worthy story with such openness that readers will turn every page rooting for her—and ultimately for all of us.

Makes Me Wanna Holler
In this "honest and searching look at the perils of growing up a black male in urban America" (*San Francisco Chronicle*), *Washington Post* reporter Nathan McCall tells the story of his passage from the street and the prison yard to the newsroom of one of America's most prestigious papers.

Heroes in Black History: True Stories from the Lives of Christian Heroes
Whether read together at family devotions or alone, *Heroes in Black History*, authored by Dave Jackson, is an ideal way to acquaint children ages six to twelve with historically important Christians while imparting valuable lessons. Featured heroes include Harriet Tubman, George Washington Carver, William Seymour, Thomas A. Dorsey, Mary McLeod Bethune, Martin Luther King Jr., and many more.

Our Lives Matter: A Queer Womanist Perspective
Our Lives Matter uses the tenor of the 2014 national protests that emerged as a response to excessive police force against black people to frame the book as following

the discursive tradition of liberation theologies broadly speaking and womanist theology specifically. Using a womanist methodological approach, Pamela R. Lightsey helps readers explore the impact of oppression against black LBTQ women while introducing them to the emergent intellectual movement known as queer theology.

The Souls of Black Folk

The Souls of Black Folk is a classic work of American literature by W. E. B. Du Bois. It is a seminal work in the history of sociology, and a cornerstone of African American literary history. Publication of *The Souls of Black Folk* was a dramatic event that helped polarize black leaders into two groups: the more conservative followers of Washington and the more radical supporters of aggressive protest. Its influence cannot be overstated. It is essential reading for everyone interested in African American history and the struggle for civil rights in America.

The New Jim Crow: Mass Incarceration in the Age of Colorblindness

This book directly challenges the notion that the election of Barack Obama signaled a new era of colorblindness. With dazzling candor, legal scholar Michelle Alexander argues that "we have not ended racial caste in America; we have merely redesigned it." By targeting black men through the War on Drugs and decimating communities of color, the US criminal justice system functions as a contemporary system of racial control—relegating millions to a permanent second-class status—even as it formally adheres to the principle of colorblindness.

Fear of the Other: No Fear of Love

In this no-nonsense book, reliable spiritual guide Will Willimon invites readers to consider the gospel command to love (and not merely tolerate) those considered to be "Other" or outside mainstream Christian culture. Rooted in the faith of Israel and the Christian story and vision, Willimon brings a Wesleyan perspective to bear on what may be the hardest thing for people of faith to do: keeping and loving the "Other" as they are—without any need for them to become like us.

Becoming an Anti-Racist Church: Journeying Toward Wholeness

Leading activist Joseph Barndt argues that Christians addressing racism in American society must begin with a frank assessment of how race figures in the churches themselves. This practical and important volume extends the insights of Barndt's earlier, more general work to address the race situation in the churches and to equip people there to be agents for change in and beyond their church communities.

"Why Are All the Black Kids Sitting Together in the Cafeteria?"

Beverly Daniel Tatum, a renowned authority on the psychology of racism, asserts that we do not know how to talk about our racial differences: whites are afraid of using the wrong words and being perceived as "racist," while parents of color are afraid of exposing their children to painful racial realities too soon. Using real-life examples and the latest research, Tatum presents strong evidence that straight talk about our racial identities—whatever they may be—is essential if we are serious about facilitating communication across racial and ethnic divides.

Articles

"The Making of Ferguson: Public Policies at the Root of Its Troubles," by Richard Rothstein, Economic Policy Institute

"The Case for Reparations," by Ta-Nehisi Coates, *The Atlantic*

"Letter from a Birmingham Jail," by Martin Luther King Jr.

"What to Say, What to Do?" by F. Willis Johnson, *Huffington Post*

"Words Matter," by Emanuel Cleaver

"Preaching to Confront Racism," by William H. Willimon

Podcasts

The Faith and Race Podcast

We Live Here Podcast

NPR's Code Switch Podcast, specifically the episode "Can We Talk About Whiteness"

Videos

"Race: The Power of an Illusion," PBS

"The Delmar Divide," BBC

"Children's Crusade," Bio.com

"Ferguson: A Report from Occupied Territory," YouTube

Please see www.AbingdonPress.com/HoldingUpYourCorner
for links to these online resources.

ABOUT THE AUTHOR

A third-generation educator, **Rev. Dr. F. Willis Johnson** is the senior minister of Wellspring Church in Ferguson, Missouri, a predominately African-American intergenerational urban parachute church plant. Thousands have been influenced by his prophetic, faith-filled reflections and strategies on social justice and racial understanding. Johnson captured national attention for his leadership in August 2014 after an unarmed African American teenager was shot and killed in Ferguson.

With more than fifteen years of professional ministry experience in Indiana, North Carolina, and Missouri, Johnson's skills extend far beyond the pulpit. Trained in education and nonprofit management, he has served in volunteer and paid leadership positions for multiple nonprofit organizations. He counsels bishops, General Board agencies, annual conferences, and local churches across the country. Additionally, Johnson serves the Drew Theological School community as the Vosburgh Visiting Professor of Ministry and Social Engagement in January 2017.

At a time when our nation is experiencing great upheaval on matters of race, policing, violence and fragmentation, Johnson continues to prepare prophetic leaders who promote healing, justice and reconciliation through his leadership of The Center for Social Empowerment. The Center is a hub for theologically informed reflection, investigation, and education on social and racial justice issues.

Nicki Reinhardt-Swierk, a contributor to this book, serves the coordinator for institutional readiness at the Center. A former educator, Harvard educated ethicist, and Walker Leadership Institute Fellow, Nicki has been involved in a variety of community organizing and uplift efforts throughout her career, focusing primarily on issues of diversity and the importance of conversation across difference. A skilled facilitator, Nicki has created and led workshops on a variety of social justice issues such as race, privilege, gender, and sexuality to audiences across the country. In addition to her work at the Center, Nicki is involved in youth and educational ministries in the St. Louis area.

EDITORIAL ACKNOWLEDGMENTS

We thank the following for their assistance in bringing *Holding Up Your Corner* to fruition:

The congregations, staff, and pastors of Pennsylvania Avenue AME Zion Church, Baltimore, Maryland, Rev. Dr. Lester McCorn; St. James UMC, Kansas City, Missouri, Rev. Dr. Emanuel Cleaver III; Providence UMC, Mt. Juliet, Tennessee, Rev. Jacob Armstrong; St Mark's Episcopal Cathedral, Seattle, Washington, Heidi Kim, The Very Reverend Steven L. Thomason, and The Reverend Canon Jennifer King Daugherty; Resurrection Downtown, Kansas City, Missouri, Rev. Scott Chrostek; The United Methodist Church of the Resurrection, Leawood, Kansas, Rev. Adam Hamilton. The Guided Conversations were field-tested at these churches, which provided immensely helpful feedback for this resource.

Eric Mattson, pastor and photographer (Missouri Conference of The United Methodist Church) for the cover photo and other photography .

Willis "Bing" Davis, artist and educator, for original artwork and creative counsel (see pages vi-vii in *Holding Up Your Corner*).

Melissa Collier Gepford, for writing (Facilitator's Guide) and editorial services.

Cris Cunningham, Redwood Pictures, for video production services.

The Center for Social Empowerment, Ferguson, Missouri, for specialized content including the privilege quiz.

And Bishop Gregory Palmer, Bishop Robert Schnase, Dottie Escobedo-Frank, and Rudy Rasmus for their counsel and encouragement.

CPSIA information can be obtained
at www.ICGtesting.com
Printed in the USA
LVOW05s0530070117
520059LV00003BD/3/P